50 Indian Dish Recipes for Home

By: Kelly Johnson

Table of Contents

- Butter Chicken
- Palak Paneer
- Chana Masala
- Rogan Josh
- Chicken Tikka Masala
- Aloo Gobi
- Tandoori Chicken
- Dal Makhani
- Baingan Bharta
- Paneer Tikka
- Masoor Dal
- Malai Kofta
- Vegetable Biryani
- Shahi Paneer
- Pav Bhaji
- Chicken Curry
- Matar Paneer
- Samosa
- Bhindi Masala
- Chicken Korma
- Rajma Masala
- Fish Curry
- Pani Puri
- Dum Aloo
- Aloo Paratha
- Keema
- Paneer Butter Masala
- Chicken 65
- Vegetable Pakora
- Dosa
- Raita
- Gajar Ka Halwa
- Chicken Biryani
- Veg Pulao
- Rasgulla

- Aloo Tikki
- Mutton Curry
- Papdi Chaat
- Chicken Chettinad
- Gobi Manchurian
- Mutton Biryani
- Chicken Saag
- Egg Curry
- Hyderabadi Biryani
- Rasam
- Gulab Jamun
- Prawn Curry
- Chicken Vindaloo
- Chicken 65
- Tomato Rasam

Butter Chicken

Ingredients:

- 500g boneless chicken, cut into bite-sized pieces
- 1 cup plain yogurt
- 2 tablespoons lemon juice
- 2 teaspoons ginger-garlic paste
- 1 teaspoon chili powder
- 1 teaspoon ground turmeric
- Salt to taste
- 2 tablespoons butter
- 1 tablespoon vegetable oil
- 2 onions, finely chopped
- 2 tomatoes, pureed
- 1 teaspoon garam masala
- 1 teaspoon ground cumin
- 1 teaspoon ground coriander
- 1/2 cup heavy cream
- Fresh cilantro leaves for garnish

Instructions:

1. In a bowl, mix together the yogurt, lemon juice, ginger-garlic paste, chili powder, turmeric, and salt. Add the chicken pieces to the marinade, making sure they are well coated. Cover and refrigerate for at least 1 hour, or overnight for best results.
2. Heat the butter and vegetable oil in a large skillet over medium heat. Add the chopped onions and cook until they turn translucent.
3. Add the marinated chicken pieces to the skillet and cook until they are browned on all sides, about 8-10 minutes.
4. Stir in the tomato puree, garam masala, ground cumin, and ground coriander. Cook for another 5 minutes, stirring occasionally.
5. Reduce the heat to low and stir in the heavy cream. Simmer for an additional 10-15 minutes, stirring occasionally, until the chicken is cooked through and the sauce has thickened.
6. Garnish with fresh cilantro leaves and serve hot with naan bread or rice.

Enjoy your homemade Butter Chicken!

Palak Paneer

Ingredients:

- 250g paneer, cubed
- 300g spinach (fresh or frozen)
- 2 tablespoons ghee or vegetable oil
- 1 onion, finely chopped
- 2 tomatoes, finely chopped
- 2 green chilies, chopped (adjust to taste)
- 1 tablespoon ginger-garlic paste
- 1 teaspoon cumin seeds
- 1 teaspoon garam masala
- 1 teaspoon ground coriander
- 1/2 teaspoon turmeric powder
- Salt to taste
- 1/2 cup heavy cream (optional)
- Fresh cilantro leaves for garnish

Instructions:

1. If using fresh spinach, wash it thoroughly and blanch it in boiling water for 2-3 minutes. Then, drain and blend it into a smooth puree. If using frozen spinach, thaw it and blend into a smooth puree.
2. Heat ghee or vegetable oil in a large skillet or pan over medium heat. Add cumin seeds and let them splutter.
3. Add chopped onions and sauté until they turn translucent.
4. Add ginger-garlic paste and chopped green chilies. Sauté for another minute.
5. Add chopped tomatoes and cook until they become soft and mushy.
6. Add garam masala, ground coriander, turmeric powder, and salt. Mix well and cook for 2-3 minutes.
7. Pour in the spinach puree and mix until well combined with the spices. Let it simmer for 5-7 minutes.
8. Add the cubed paneer to the spinach mixture and gently mix.
9. If using heavy cream, pour it into the pan and stir until well incorporated. Simmer for another 2-3 minutes.
10. Garnish with fresh cilantro leaves.

11. Serve hot with naan bread or rice.

Enjoy your homemade Palak Paneer!

Chana Masala

Ingredients:

- 2 cups dried chickpeas (or 2 cans, drained and rinsed)
- 2 tablespoons vegetable oil
- 1 onion, finely chopped
- 3 cloves garlic, minced
- 1-inch piece of ginger, grated
- 2 green chilies, finely chopped (optional)
- 2 tomatoes, finely chopped
- 2 teaspoons ground cumin
- 2 teaspoons ground coriander
- 1 teaspoon turmeric powder
- 1 teaspoon garam masala
- 1 teaspoon paprika (optional, for extra color)
- Salt to taste
- 1 cup water
- Fresh cilantro leaves for garnish

Instructions:

1. If using dried chickpeas, soak them overnight in water. Drain and rinse them before cooking. If using canned chickpeas, drain and rinse them.
2. Heat vegetable oil in a large skillet or pot over medium heat. Add chopped onions and sauté until they turn translucent.
3. Add minced garlic, grated ginger, and chopped green chilies. Sauté for another minute until fragrant.
4. Add chopped tomatoes to the skillet and cook until they become soft and mushy.
5. Stir in ground cumin, ground coriander, turmeric powder, garam masala, paprika (if using), and salt. Mix well and cook for 2-3 minutes to let the spices toast and release their flavors.
6. Add the soaked and drained chickpeas to the skillet. Stir until the chickpeas are coated with the spice mixture.
7. Pour in 1 cup of water and bring the mixture to a simmer. Cover and cook for 20-25 minutes, stirring occasionally, until the chickpeas are tender and the flavors are well combined.
8. Adjust salt and spices according to your taste preferences.

9. Garnish with fresh cilantro leaves before serving.
10. Serve hot with rice, naan bread, or roti.

Enjoy your homemade Chana Masala!

Rogan Josh

Ingredients:

- 500g lamb, cut into cubes
- 3 tablespoons vegetable oil or ghee
- 2 onions, finely chopped
- 3 cloves garlic, minced
- 1-inch piece of ginger, grated
- 2 green chilies, chopped (optional)
- 2 tomatoes, finely chopped or pureed
- 1 teaspoon cumin seeds
- 4 green cardamom pods
- 2 black cardamom pods
- 2 cloves
- 1 cinnamon stick
- 1 teaspoon ground coriander
- 1 teaspoon ground cumin
- 1 teaspoon ground turmeric
- 1 teaspoon paprika
- 1 teaspoon Kashmiri red chili powder (adjust to taste)
- 1 teaspoon garam masala
- Salt to taste
- 1/2 cup plain yogurt
- Fresh cilantro leaves for garnish

Instructions:

1. Heat vegetable oil or ghee in a large pot or pressure cooker over medium heat. Add cumin seeds and let them splutter.
2. Add chopped onions and sauté until they turn golden brown.
3. Add minced garlic, grated ginger, and chopped green chilies. Sauté for another 2-3 minutes until fragrant.
4. Add chopped tomatoes or tomato puree to the pot. Cook until they become soft and mushy.
5. Add whole green cardamom pods, black cardamom pods, cloves, and cinnamon stick to the pot. Stir well.

6. Stir in ground coriander, ground cumin, ground turmeric, paprika, Kashmiri red chili powder, and salt. Mix until well combined with the onion-tomato mixture.
7. Add the cubed lamb to the pot and stir until it is coated with the spice mixture.
8. Pour in the plain yogurt and mix well. Ensure that the yogurt is well incorporated into the sauce.
9. If using a pressure cooker, add about 1/2 cup of water. Close the lid and cook for about 20-25 minutes, or until the lamb is tender. If using a regular pot, add enough water to cover the lamb, then simmer, covered, for 1 to 1.5 hours until the lamb is tender.
10. Once the lamb is cooked, sprinkle garam masala over the dish and mix well.
11. Garnish with fresh cilantro leaves before serving.
12. Serve hot with rice or naan bread.

Enjoy your homemade Rogan Josh!

Chicken Tikka Masala

Ingredients:

For the Chicken Tikka:

- 500g boneless, skinless chicken breasts or thighs, cut into bite-sized pieces
- 1 cup plain yogurt
- 2 tablespoons lemon juice
- 2 teaspoons ginger-garlic paste
- 1 teaspoon ground cumin
- 1 teaspoon ground coriander
- 1 teaspoon paprika
- 1/2 teaspoon turmeric powder
- 1/2 teaspoon garam masala
- 1/2 teaspoon salt
- Vegetable oil for grilling or broiling

For the Masala Sauce:

- 2 tablespoons vegetable oil or ghee
- 1 onion, finely chopped
- 3 cloves garlic, minced
- 1-inch piece of ginger, grated
- 2 green chilies, chopped (adjust to taste)
- 2 tomatoes, finely chopped or pureed
- 1 teaspoon ground cumin
- 1 teaspoon ground coriander
- 1 teaspoon paprika
- 1 teaspoon garam masala
- 1/2 teaspoon turmeric powder
- 1/2 cup heavy cream
- Salt to taste
- Fresh cilantro leaves for garnish

Instructions:

1. In a bowl, mix together yogurt, lemon juice, ginger-garlic paste, ground cumin, ground coriander, paprika, turmeric powder, garam masala, and salt. Add chicken pieces and toss until well coated. Cover and marinate in the refrigerator for at least 1 hour, or overnight for best results.
2. Preheat the grill or broiler. Thread the marinated chicken pieces onto skewers and grill or broil until cooked through and slightly charred, about 10-12 minutes, turning occasionally. Remove from heat and set aside.
3. Heat vegetable oil or ghee in a large skillet over medium heat. Add chopped onions and sauté until they turn translucent.
4. Add minced garlic, grated ginger, and chopped green chilies. Sauté for another 2-3 minutes until fragrant.
5. Add chopped tomatoes or tomato puree to the skillet. Cook until they become soft and mushy.
6. Stir in ground cumin, ground coriander, paprika, garam masala, turmeric powder, and salt. Mix well and cook for 2-3 minutes to let the spices toast and release their flavors.
7. Add the grilled chicken tikka pieces to the skillet and stir until they are well coated with the masala sauce.
8. Pour in the heavy cream and stir until well combined. Simmer for another 5-7 minutes, stirring occasionally, until the sauce thickens.
9. Adjust salt and spices according to your taste preferences.
10. Garnish with fresh cilantro leaves before serving.
11. Serve hot with rice or naan bread.

Enjoy your homemade Chicken Tikka Masala!

Aloo Gobi

Ingredients:

- 1 medium-sized cauliflower, cut into florets
- 2 medium-sized potatoes, peeled and cut into cubes
- 2 tablespoons vegetable oil
- 1 teaspoon cumin seeds
- 1 onion, finely chopped
- 2 tomatoes, finely chopped or pureed
- 2 green chilies, chopped (adjust to taste)
- 1 teaspoon ginger-garlic paste
- 1 teaspoon ground turmeric
- 1 teaspoon ground cumin
- 1 teaspoon ground coriander
- 1/2 teaspoon red chili powder (adjust to taste)
- Salt to taste
- Fresh cilantro leaves for garnish

Instructions:

1. Heat vegetable oil in a large skillet or pan over medium heat. Add cumin seeds and let them splutter.
2. Add chopped onions and sauté until they turn translucent.
3. Add ginger-garlic paste and chopped green chilies. Sauté for another minute until fragrant.
4. Add chopped tomatoes or tomato puree to the skillet. Cook until they become soft and mushy.
5. Stir in ground turmeric, ground cumin, ground coriander, red chili powder, and salt. Mix well and cook for 2-3 minutes to let the spices toast and release their flavors.
6. Add cauliflower florets and potato cubes to the skillet. Stir until they are well coated with the spice mixture.
7. Cover the skillet and cook on medium-low heat for about 15-20 minutes, or until the cauliflower and potatoes are tender, stirring occasionally. If needed, you can add a splash of water to prevent sticking and to help cook the vegetables evenly.

8. Once the cauliflower and potatoes are cooked through, uncover the skillet and cook for an additional 5-7 minutes to let any excess moisture evaporate and to allow the flavors to meld together.
9. Adjust salt and spices according to your taste preferences.
10. Garnish with fresh cilantro leaves before serving.
11. Serve hot with rice or roti.

Enjoy your homemade Aloo Gobi!

Tandoori Chicken

Ingredients:

- 4 chicken leg quarters or 8 chicken thighs, skin-on and bone-in
- 1 cup plain yogurt
- 2 tablespoons lemon juice
- 2 tablespoons vegetable oil
- 1 tablespoon ginger-garlic paste
- 2 teaspoons ground cumin
- 2 teaspoons ground coriander
- 2 teaspoons paprika
- 1 teaspoon ground turmeric
- 1 teaspoon garam masala
- 1 teaspoon ground Kashmiri red chili powder (adjust to taste)
- 1/2 teaspoon ground black pepper
- 1/2 teaspoon salt (adjust to taste)
- Lemon wedges and fresh cilantro leaves for garnish

Instructions:

1. Rinse the chicken pieces under cold water and pat them dry with paper towels. Make 2-3 deep slashes on each piece to allow the marinade to penetrate.
2. In a bowl, mix together yogurt, lemon juice, vegetable oil, ginger-garlic paste, ground cumin, ground coriander, paprika, ground turmeric, garam masala, Kashmiri red chili powder, black pepper, and salt until well combined.
3. Add the chicken pieces to the marinade and toss until they are well coated. Cover the bowl and refrigerate for at least 2 hours, or preferably overnight, to allow the flavors to meld together.
4. Preheat your grill to medium-high heat. If using a charcoal grill, set up for indirect grilling.
5. Remove the chicken from the marinade and shake off any excess. Reserve the remaining marinade for basting.
6. Grill the chicken pieces over direct heat, skin-side down, for 5-7 minutes or until the skin is charred and crispy. Flip the chicken pieces and grill for another 5-7 minutes on the other side.

7. Move the chicken pieces to the cooler, indirect heat side of the grill. Baste them with the reserved marinade and continue to cook, covered, for another 15-20 minutes, or until the chicken is cooked through and juices run clear. The internal temperature should reach 165°F (75°C).
8. Once cooked, remove the chicken from the grill and let it rest for a few minutes.
9. Garnish with lemon wedges and fresh cilantro leaves before serving.
10. Serve hot with naan bread, rice, or your favorite side dishes.

Enjoy your homemade Tandoori Chicken!

Dal Makhani

Ingredients:

- 1 cup whole black lentils (urad dal)
- 1/4 cup kidney beans (rajma)
- 4 cups water
- 2 tablespoons ghee or butter
- 1 onion, finely chopped
- 3 cloves garlic, minced
- 1-inch piece of ginger, grated
- 2 green chilies, chopped (adjust to taste)
- 2 tomatoes, finely chopped or pureed
- 1 teaspoon cumin seeds
- 1 teaspoon garam masala
- 1/2 teaspoon ground turmeric
- 1/2 teaspoon ground coriander
- 1/4 teaspoon ground cinnamon
- 1/4 teaspoon ground cloves
- Salt to taste
- 1/2 cup cream
- Fresh cilantro leaves for garnish

Instructions:

1. Rinse the black lentils (urad dal) and kidney beans (rajma) under cold water. Soak them together in water for at least 6 hours or overnight.
2. Drain the soaked lentils and beans. Transfer them to a pressure cooker or a large pot. Add 4 cups of water and cook until they are soft and fully cooked. If using a pressure cooker, cook for about 20-25 minutes after reaching full pressure. If using a regular pot, cook for about 1.5 to 2 hours, or until tender.
3. Once the lentils and beans are cooked, mash them slightly with the back of a spoon or a potato masher. Set aside.
4. In a separate large skillet or pan, heat ghee or butter over medium heat. Add cumin seeds and let them splutter.
5. Add chopped onions and sauté until they turn translucent.

6. Add minced garlic, grated ginger, and chopped green chilies. Sauté for another 2-3 minutes until fragrant.
7. Add chopped tomatoes or tomato puree to the skillet. Cook until they become soft and mushy.
8. Stir in garam masala, ground turmeric, ground coriander, ground cinnamon, and ground cloves. Mix well and cook for 2-3 minutes to let the spices toast and release their flavors.
9. Add the cooked lentils and beans to the skillet. Mix until they are well combined with the spice mixture.
10. Pour in the cream and stir until well incorporated. Simmer for another 10-15 minutes, stirring occasionally, until the flavors meld together and the dal thickens.
11. Adjust salt according to your taste preferences.
12. Garnish with fresh cilantro leaves before serving.
13. Serve hot with rice, naan bread, or roti.

Enjoy your homemade Dal Makhani!

Baingan Bharta

Ingredients:

- 2 large eggplants (brinjals/aubergines)
- 2 tablespoons vegetable oil
- 1 teaspoon cumin seeds
- 1 onion, finely chopped
- 2 tomatoes, finely chopped
- 3 cloves garlic, minced
- 1-inch piece of ginger, grated
- 2 green chilies, chopped (adjust to taste)
- 1 teaspoon ground coriander
- 1/2 teaspoon ground turmeric
- 1/2 teaspoon red chili powder (adjust to taste)
- Salt to taste
- Fresh cilantro leaves for garnish

Instructions:

1. Preheat your oven to 400°F (200°C). Prick the eggplants with a fork and roast them on a baking sheet in the oven for about 30-40 minutes, or until they are completely soft and the skin is charred. Alternatively, you can roast them directly over a gas flame until the skin is charred and the flesh is soft.
2. Once the eggplants are cooked, remove them from the oven or flame and let them cool slightly. Peel off the charred skin and discard. Mash the flesh using a fork or potato masher. Set aside.
3. Heat vegetable oil in a large skillet or pan over medium heat. Add cumin seeds and let them splutter.
4. Add chopped onions to the skillet and sauté until they turn translucent.
5. Add minced garlic, grated ginger, and chopped green chilies. Sauté for another 2-3 minutes until fragrant.
6. Add chopped tomatoes to the skillet and cook until they become soft and mushy.
7. Stir in ground coriander, ground turmeric, red chili powder, and salt. Mix well and cook for 2-3 minutes to let the spices toast and release their flavors.
8. Add the mashed eggplant to the skillet and mix until it is well combined with the spice mixture.

9. Simmer the mixture for 5-7 minutes, stirring occasionally, to allow the flavors to meld together and the excess moisture to evaporate.
10. Adjust salt and spices according to your taste preferences.
11. Garnish with fresh cilantro leaves before serving.
12. Serve hot with rice or roti.

Enjoy your homemade Baingan Bharta!

Paneer Tikka

Ingredients:

- 250g paneer, cut into cubes
- 1 bell pepper (capsicum), cut into chunks
- 1 onion, cut into chunks
- 1 cup plain yogurt
- 2 tablespoons lemon juice
- 1 tablespoon ginger-garlic paste
- 1 teaspoon ground cumin
- 1 teaspoon ground coriander
- 1 teaspoon paprika
- 1/2 teaspoon turmeric powder
- 1/2 teaspoon garam masala
- 1/2 teaspoon chaat masala (optional)
- Salt to taste
- Vegetable oil for grilling or broiling
- Skewers (if using wooden skewers, soak them in water for 30 minutes)

Instructions:

1. In a bowl, mix together yogurt, lemon juice, ginger-garlic paste, ground cumin, ground coriander, paprika, turmeric powder, garam masala, chaat masala (if using), and salt until well combined.
2. Add paneer cubes, bell pepper chunks, and onion chunks to the marinade. Toss until they are well coated. Cover the bowl and refrigerate for at least 1 hour, or preferably overnight, to allow the flavors to meld together.
3. Preheat your grill to medium-high heat. If using a charcoal grill, set up for direct grilling.
4. Remove the paneer cubes, bell pepper chunks, and onion chunks from the marinade and thread them onto skewers, alternating between paneer, bell pepper, and onion.
5. Brush the grill grates with vegetable oil to prevent sticking. Place the skewers on the grill and cook for 3-4 minutes on each side, or until they are charred and slightly crispy.

6. Once cooked, remove the skewers from the grill and transfer the paneer tikka to a serving plate.
7. Serve hot with mint chutney, sliced onions, and lemon wedges on the side.

Enjoy your homemade Paneer Tikka!

Masoor Dal

Ingredients:

- 1 cup masoor dal (red lentils)
- 3 cups water
- 1 tablespoon vegetable oil or ghee
- 1 teaspoon cumin seeds
- 1 onion, finely chopped
- 3 cloves garlic, minced
- 1-inch piece of ginger, grated
- 2 tomatoes, finely chopped or pureed
- 1 green chili, chopped (adjust to taste)
- 1 teaspoon ground turmeric
- 1 teaspoon ground coriander
- 1/2 teaspoon red chili powder (adjust to taste)
- Salt to taste
- Fresh cilantro leaves for garnish
- Lemon wedges for serving (optional)

Instructions:

1. Rinse the masoor dal under cold water until the water runs clear. Drain well.
2. In a large pot, combine the masoor dal and water. Bring to a boil over medium-high heat. Once boiling, reduce the heat to low, cover partially, and simmer for about 20-25 minutes, or until the dal is soft and mushy. Stir occasionally and add more water if needed to achieve your desired consistency.
3. Once the dal is cooked, use a whisk or the back of a spoon to mash it slightly. Set aside.
4. In a separate pan, heat vegetable oil or ghee over medium heat. Add cumin seeds and let them splutter.
5. Add chopped onions to the pan and sauté until they turn translucent.
6. Add minced garlic, grated ginger, and chopped green chili. Sauté for another 2-3 minutes until fragrant.
7. Add chopped tomatoes or tomato puree to the pan. Cook until they become soft and mushy.

8. Stir in ground turmeric, ground coriander, red chili powder, and salt. Mix well and cook for 2-3 minutes to let the spices toast and release their flavors.
9. Add the cooked masoor dal to the pan and mix until well combined with the spice mixture. Simmer for another 5-7 minutes to allow the flavors to meld together.
10. Adjust salt and spices according to your taste preferences.
11. Garnish with fresh cilantro leaves before serving.
12. Serve hot with rice or roti. Optionally, serve with lemon wedges on the side for squeezing over the dal.

Enjoy your homemade Masoor Dal!

Malai Kofta

Ingredients:

For the Koftas:

- 2 large potatoes, boiled and mashed
- 1 cup paneer, grated
- 2 tablespoons corn flour or all-purpose flour
- 1 teaspoon ginger-garlic paste
- 1/2 teaspoon garam masala
- Salt to taste
- Vegetable oil for frying

For the Gravy:

- 2 tablespoons vegetable oil or ghee
- 1 onion, finely chopped
- 2 tomatoes, finely chopped or pureed
- 1 tablespoon ginger-garlic paste
- 1 teaspoon ground cumin
- 1 teaspoon ground coriander
- 1/2 teaspoon turmeric powder
- 1/2 teaspoon red chili powder (adjust to taste)
- 1/2 cup cashew nuts, soaked in warm water for 30 minutes and blended into a smooth paste
- 1/2 cup heavy cream
- Salt to taste
- Fresh cilantro leaves for garnish

Instructions:

1. To make the koftas, in a large bowl, combine mashed potatoes, grated paneer, corn flour or all-purpose flour, ginger-garlic paste, garam masala, and salt. Mix well until everything is thoroughly combined.
2. Divide the mixture into equal portions and shape each portion into round balls or oval shapes to form koftas.

3. Heat vegetable oil in a deep frying pan over medium heat. Once the oil is hot, carefully add the koftas in batches and fry until they are golden brown and crispy on all sides. Remove them from the oil using a slotted spoon and drain on paper towels. Set aside.
4. To make the gravy, heat vegetable oil or ghee in a large skillet or pan over medium heat. Add chopped onions and sauté until they turn translucent.
5. Add ginger-garlic paste to the skillet and sauté for another minute until fragrant.
6. Add chopped tomatoes or tomato puree to the skillet. Cook until they become soft and mushy.
7. Stir in ground cumin, ground coriander, turmeric powder, and red chili powder. Mix well and cook for 2-3 minutes to let the spices toast and release their flavors.
8. Add the cashew nut paste to the skillet and mix until well combined with the spice mixture. Cook for another 2-3 minutes.
9. Pour in the heavy cream and stir until well incorporated. Simmer for 5-7 minutes, stirring occasionally, until the gravy thickens.
10. Adjust salt according to your taste preferences.
11. Gently add the fried koftas to the gravy and simmer for another 5 minutes, allowing the koftas to absorb the flavors of the gravy.
12. Garnish with fresh cilantro leaves before serving.
13. Serve hot with rice or naan bread.

Enjoy your homemade Malai Kofta!

Vegetable Biryani

Ingredients:

For the Rice:

- 2 cups Basmati rice, soaked in water for 30 minutes and drained
- 4 cups water
- 2 tablespoons ghee or vegetable oil
- 1 bay leaf
- 2-3 green cardamom pods
- 2-3 cloves
- 1-inch cinnamon stick
- Salt to taste

For the Vegetable Mixture:

- 2 tablespoons ghee or vegetable oil
- 1 onion, thinly sliced
- 2 carrots, diced
- 1 cup green beans, chopped
- 1 cup cauliflower florets
- 1 cup green peas (fresh or frozen)
- 1 bell pepper (capsicum), diced
- 1 tomato, diced
- 1 tablespoon ginger-garlic paste
- 1 teaspoon ground turmeric
- 1 teaspoon ground cumin
- 1 teaspoon ground coriander
- 1 teaspoon garam masala
- Salt to taste
- Fresh cilantro leaves for garnish

Instructions:

1. In a large pot, bring 4 cups of water to a boil. Add the soaked and drained Basmati rice, ghee or vegetable oil, bay leaf, green cardamom pods, cloves, cinnamon stick, and salt. Stir gently and let it cook until the rice is 70-80% cooked. Drain the rice and set aside.
2. In a separate large skillet or pan, heat ghee or vegetable oil over medium heat. Add sliced onions and sauté until they turn translucent.
3. Add diced carrots, chopped green beans, cauliflower florets, green peas, diced bell pepper, and diced tomato to the skillet. Sauté for 5-7 minutes until the vegetables are slightly tender.
4. Stir in ginger-garlic paste and sauté for another minute until fragrant.
5. Add ground turmeric, ground cumin, ground coriander, garam masala, and salt. Mix well and cook for 2-3 minutes to let the spices toast and release their flavors.
6. Gently fold in the partially cooked Basmati rice with the vegetable mixture, taking care not to break the rice grains. Ensure that the vegetables and rice are evenly distributed.
7. Cover the skillet with a tight-fitting lid and cook on low heat for another 10-15 minutes, allowing the flavors to meld together and the rice to fully cook.
8. Once the rice and vegetables are fully cooked, remove the skillet from heat and let it sit, covered, for another 5 minutes.
9. Garnish with fresh cilantro leaves before serving.
10. Serve hot with raita (yogurt dip) or your favorite side dish.

Enjoy your homemade Vegetable Biryani!

Shahi Paneer

Ingredients:

- 250g paneer, cut into cubes
- 2 tablespoons ghee or vegetable oil
- 1 onion, finely chopped
- 2 tomatoes, finely chopped or pureed
- 1 tablespoon ginger-garlic paste
- 1 teaspoon ground turmeric
- 1 teaspoon ground cumin
- 1 teaspoon ground coriander
- 1/2 teaspoon red chili powder (adjust to taste)
- 1/2 teaspoon garam masala
- 1/2 cup cashew nuts, soaked in warm water for 30 minutes and blended into a smooth paste
- 1/4 cup heavy cream
- 1/4 cup milk
- Salt to taste
- Fresh cilantro leaves for garnish

Instructions:

1. Heat ghee or vegetable oil in a large skillet or pan over medium heat. Add chopped onions and sauté until they turn translucent.
2. Add ginger-garlic paste to the skillet and sauté for another minute until fragrant.
3. Add chopped tomatoes or tomato puree to the skillet. Cook until they become soft and mushy.
4. Stir in ground turmeric, ground cumin, ground coriander, red chili powder, and garam masala. Mix well and cook for 2-3 minutes to let the spices toast and release their flavors.
5. Add the cashew nut paste to the skillet and mix until well combined with the spice mixture. Cook for another 2-3 minutes.
6. Pour in the heavy cream and milk. Stir until well incorporated and simmer for 5-7 minutes, stirring occasionally, until the gravy thickens.

7. Add the paneer cubes to the skillet and gently mix until they are coated with the gravy. Simmer for another 2-3 minutes to allow the paneer to absorb the flavors of the gravy.
8. Adjust salt according to your taste preferences.
9. Garnish with fresh cilantro leaves before serving.
10. Serve hot with rice, naan bread, or roti.

Enjoy your homemade Shahi Paneer!

Pav Bhaji

Ingredients:

For the Bhaji:

- 3 large potatoes, boiled and mashed
- 1 cup cauliflower florets, boiled and mashed
- 1 cup green peas, boiled and mashed
- 1 cup carrots, finely chopped and boiled
- 1 onion, finely chopped
- 1 bell pepper (capsicum), finely chopped
- 2 tomatoes, finely chopped
- 4 cloves garlic, minced
- 1-inch piece of ginger, grated
- 2 green chilies, finely chopped (adjust to taste)
- 2 tablespoons butter or ghee
- 2 tablespoons pav bhaji masala
- 1 teaspoon red chili powder (adjust to taste)
- 1 teaspoon ground turmeric
- Salt to taste
- Fresh cilantro leaves for garnish
- Lemon wedges for serving
- Pav (bread rolls) for serving

Instructions:

1. In a large pan or skillet, melt butter or ghee over medium heat.
2. Add minced garlic, grated ginger, and chopped green chilies. Sauté for a minute until fragrant.
3. Add chopped onions to the skillet and cook until they turn translucent.
4. Add chopped bell pepper and sauté for a few minutes until it becomes soft.
5. Add chopped tomatoes to the skillet and cook until they become soft and mushy.
6. Stir in pav bhaji masala, red chili powder, ground turmeric, and salt. Mix well and cook for a couple of minutes to let the spices toast and release their flavors.
7. Add mashed potatoes, cauliflower, green peas, and carrots to the skillet. Mix well until all the vegetables are combined with the spice mixture.

8. Using a potato masher or the back of a spoon, mash the vegetables until they are well incorporated and reach the desired consistency. You can add a little water if the mixture is too thick.
9. Simmer the bhaji for 5-10 minutes, stirring occasionally, to allow the flavors to meld together.
10. Garnish with fresh cilantro leaves before serving.
11. Heat the pav (bread rolls) on a skillet with a little butter until they are warm and slightly toasted.
12. Serve the pav bhaji hot with a dollop of butter, lemon wedges, and additional chopped onions and cilantro on the side.

Enjoy your homemade Pav Bhaji!

Chicken Curry

Ingredients:

- 500g chicken pieces (bone-in or boneless)
- 2 tablespoons vegetable oil
- 1 onion, finely chopped
- 3 cloves garlic, minced
- 1-inch piece of ginger, grated
- 2 tomatoes, finely chopped or pureed
- 2 green chilies, slit (adjust to taste)
- 1 teaspoon ground turmeric
- 2 teaspoons ground coriander
- 1 teaspoon ground cumin
- 1 teaspoon red chili powder (adjust to taste)
- 1 teaspoon garam masala
- Salt to taste
- 1/2 cup water or chicken stock
- Fresh cilantro leaves for garnish

Instructions:

1. Heat vegetable oil in a large skillet or pan over medium heat. Add chopped onions and sauté until they turn translucent.
2. Add minced garlic and grated ginger to the skillet. Sauté for another minute until fragrant.
3. Add chopped tomatoes or tomato puree to the skillet. Cook until they become soft and mushy.
4. Stir in ground turmeric, ground coriander, ground cumin, red chili powder, garam masala, and salt. Mix well and cook for 2-3 minutes to let the spices toast and release their flavors.
5. Add chicken pieces to the skillet and stir until they are well coated with the spice mixture.
6. Pour in water or chicken stock and stir to combine. Bring the mixture to a simmer.
7. Cover the skillet and cook on low heat for about 20-25 minutes, or until the chicken is cooked through and tender, stirring occasionally.

8. Once the chicken is cooked, adjust salt and spices according to your taste preferences.
9. Garnish with fresh cilantro leaves before serving.
10. Serve hot with rice, naan bread, or roti.

Enjoy your homemade Chicken Curry! You can also customize this recipe by adding other ingredients like coconut milk, yogurt, or various vegetables.

Matar Paneer

Ingredients:

- 250g paneer, cut into cubes
- 1 cup green peas (fresh or frozen)
- 2 tablespoons vegetable oil or ghee
- 1 onion, finely chopped
- 2 tomatoes, finely chopped or pureed
- 3 cloves garlic, minced
- 1-inch piece of ginger, grated
- 2 green chilies, chopped (adjust to taste)
- 1 teaspoon cumin seeds
- 1 teaspoon ground turmeric
- 1 teaspoon ground coriander
- 1 teaspoon red chili powder (adjust to taste)
- 1/2 teaspoon garam masala
- Salt to taste
- 1/2 cup water
- Fresh cilantro leaves for garnish

Instructions:

1. Heat vegetable oil or ghee in a large skillet or pan over medium heat. Add cumin seeds and let them splutter.
2. Add chopped onions to the skillet and sauté until they turn translucent.
3. Add minced garlic, grated ginger, and chopped green chilies. Sauté for another 2-3 minutes until fragrant.
4. Add chopped tomatoes or tomato puree to the skillet. Cook until they become soft and mushy.
5. Stir in ground turmeric, ground coriander, red chili powder, garam masala, and salt. Mix well and cook for 2-3 minutes to let the spices toast and release their flavors.
6. Add green peas to the skillet and mix until they are well coated with the spice mixture.
7. Pour in water and stir to combine. Bring the mixture to a simmer.

8. Cover the skillet and cook on low heat for about 10-15 minutes, or until the peas are tender and cooked through.
9. Once the peas are cooked, add the paneer cubes to the skillet and gently mix until they are heated through.
10. Adjust salt and spices according to your taste preferences.
11. Garnish with fresh cilantro leaves before serving.
12. Serve hot with rice, naan bread, or roti.

Enjoy your homemade Matar Paneer!

Samosa

Ingredients:

For the dough:

- 2 cups all-purpose flour
- 1/2 teaspoon salt
- 1/4 cup vegetable oil or ghee
- Water, as needed

For the filling:

- 2 medium potatoes, boiled, peeled, and mashed
- 1 cup green peas (fresh or frozen), boiled
- 1 onion, finely chopped
- 2 green chilies, finely chopped (adjust to taste)
- 1 teaspoon cumin seeds
- 1 teaspoon coriander seeds, crushed
- 1 teaspoon ginger-garlic paste
- 1/2 teaspoon turmeric powder
- 1 teaspoon ground cumin
- 1 teaspoon ground coriander
- 1/2 teaspoon garam masala
- Salt to taste
- 2 tablespoons vegetable oil or ghee
- Fresh cilantro leaves, chopped
- Vegetable oil for frying

Instructions:

1. To make the dough, combine the all-purpose flour and salt in a mixing bowl. Add vegetable oil or ghee and rub it into the flour mixture until it resembles breadcrumbs.

2. Gradually add water, a little at a time, and knead until you have a smooth and pliable dough. Cover the dough with a damp cloth and let it rest for at least 30 minutes.
3. To make the filling, heat vegetable oil or ghee in a large skillet or pan over medium heat. Add cumin seeds and crushed coriander seeds. Let them splutter.
4. Add chopped onions and sauté until they turn translucent.
5. Add ginger-garlic paste and chopped green chilies. Sauté for another minute until fragrant.
6. Add turmeric powder, ground cumin, ground coriander, garam masala, and salt. Mix well.
7. Add boiled and mashed potatoes and boiled green peas to the skillet. Mix until well combined with the spice mixture. Cook for 3-4 minutes, stirring occasionally.
8. Stir in chopped fresh cilantro leaves. Remove the filling from heat and let it cool completely.
9. Divide the dough into small lemon-sized balls. Roll out each ball into a thin circle (approximately 6-7 inches in diameter).
10. Cut each circle in half to form semi-circles.
11. Take one semi-circle and fold it into a cone shape, sealing the edges with a little water.
12. Fill the cone with a spoonful of the cooled filling.
13. Seal the open end of the cone by folding and pressing the edges together.
14. Repeat the process with the remaining dough and filling to make all the samosas.
15. Heat vegetable oil in a deep frying pan over medium heat. Once the oil is hot, fry the samosas in batches until they are golden brown and crispy on all sides.
16. Remove the fried samosas from the oil using a slotted spoon and drain on paper towels.
17. Serve hot with mint chutney or tamarind chutney.

Enjoy your homemade vegetable samosas!

Bhindi Masala

Ingredients:

- 500g okra (bhindi), washed, dried, and cut into 1-inch pieces
- 2 tablespoons vegetable oil
- 1 teaspoon cumin seeds
- 1 onion, thinly sliced
- 2 tomatoes, finely chopped or pureed
- 3 cloves garlic, minced
- 1-inch piece of ginger, grated
- 2 green chilies, chopped (adjust to taste)
- 1 teaspoon ground coriander
- 1/2 teaspoon ground turmeric
- 1/2 teaspoon red chili powder (adjust to taste)
- 1/2 teaspoon ground cumin
- 1/2 teaspoon garam masala
- Salt to taste
- Fresh cilantro leaves for garnish
- Lemon wedges for serving (optional)

Instructions:

1. Heat vegetable oil in a large skillet or pan over medium heat. Add cumin seeds and let them splutter.
2. Add thinly sliced onions to the skillet and sauté until they turn translucent.
3. Add minced garlic, grated ginger, and chopped green chilies. Sauté for another 2-3 minutes until fragrant.
4. Add chopped tomatoes or tomato puree to the skillet. Cook until they become soft and mushy.
5. Stir in ground coriander, ground turmeric, red chili powder, ground cumin, garam masala, and salt. Mix well and cook for 2-3 minutes to let the spices toast and release their flavors.
6. Add the chopped okra (bhindi) to the skillet and mix until it is well coated with the spice mixture.
7. Cover the skillet and cook on low heat for about 15-20 minutes, stirring occasionally, or until the okra is tender and cooked through.

8. Once the okra is cooked, adjust salt and spices according to your taste preferences.
9. Garnish with fresh cilantro leaves before serving.
10. Serve hot with roti, naan bread, or rice.
11. Optionally, serve with lemon wedges on the side for squeezing over the bhindi masala.

Enjoy your homemade Bhindi Masala!

Chicken Korma

Ingredients:

- 500g chicken pieces, bone-in or boneless
- 2 tablespoons vegetable oil or ghee
- 1 onion, finely chopped
- 2 tomatoes, finely chopped or pureed
- 3 cloves garlic, minced
- 1-inch piece of ginger, grated
- 2 green chilies, chopped (adjust to taste)
- 1/2 cup plain yogurt
- 1/4 cup cashew nuts, soaked in warm water for 30 minutes and blended into a smooth paste
- 1/4 cup heavy cream
- 1 teaspoon ground turmeric
- 1 teaspoon ground coriander
- 1/2 teaspoon ground cumin
- 1/2 teaspoon red chili powder (adjust to taste)
- 1/2 teaspoon garam masala
- Salt to taste
- Fresh cilantro leaves for garnish

Instructions:

1. Heat vegetable oil or ghee in a large skillet or pan over medium heat. Add chopped onions and sauté until they turn translucent.
2. Add minced garlic, grated ginger, and chopped green chilies. Sauté for another 2-3 minutes until fragrant.
3. Add chopped tomatoes or tomato puree to the skillet. Cook until they become soft and mushy.
4. Stir in ground turmeric, ground coriander, ground cumin, red chili powder, and garam masala. Mix well and cook for 2-3 minutes to let the spices toast and release their flavors.
5. Add chicken pieces to the skillet and mix until they are well coated with the spice mixture.
6. Cook the chicken until it is lightly browned on all sides.

7. In a separate bowl, whisk together plain yogurt and cashew nut paste until smooth.
8. Pour the yogurt mixture into the skillet and stir until well combined with the chicken and spice mixture.
9. Reduce the heat to low and simmer for about 15-20 minutes, or until the chicken is cooked through and tender, stirring occasionally.
10. Stir in heavy cream and simmer for another 2-3 minutes.
11. Adjust salt and spices according to your taste preferences.
12. Garnish with fresh cilantro leaves before serving.
13. Serve hot with rice, naan bread, or roti.

Enjoy your homemade Chicken Korma!

Rajma Masala

Ingredients:

- 1 cup dried kidney beans (rajma), soaked overnight in water
- 2 tablespoons vegetable oil
- 1 onion, finely chopped
- 3 cloves garlic, minced
- 1-inch piece of ginger, grated
- 2 tomatoes, finely chopped or pureed
- 2 green chilies, slit (adjust to taste)
- 1 teaspoon cumin seeds
- 1 teaspoon ground coriander
- 1/2 teaspoon ground turmeric
- 1/2 teaspoon red chili powder (adjust to taste)
- 1/2 teaspoon garam masala
- Salt to taste
- Fresh cilantro leaves for garnish

Instructions:

1. Rinse the soaked kidney beans under cold water and drain well.
2. In a pressure cooker or large pot, add the soaked kidney beans along with fresh water. Bring to a boil, then reduce the heat to low and simmer until the beans are cooked through and tender. If using a pressure cooker, cook for about 15-20 minutes after reaching full pressure. If using a pot, it may take around 1 to 1.5 hours to cook.
3. Once the kidney beans are cooked, drain any excess water and set them aside.
4. In a large skillet or pan, heat vegetable oil over medium heat. Add cumin seeds and let them splutter.
5. Add chopped onions to the skillet and sauté until they turn translucent.
6. Add minced garlic and grated ginger to the skillet. Sauté for another minute until fragrant.
7. Add chopped tomatoes or tomato puree to the skillet. Cook until they become soft and mushy.
8. Stir in ground coriander, ground turmeric, red chili powder, and garam masala. Mix well and cook for 2-3 minutes to let the spices toast and release their flavors.

9. Add the cooked kidney beans to the skillet and mix until they are well coated with the spice mixture.
10. Add salt to taste and adjust the consistency of the gravy by adding water if necessary. Simmer for 10-15 minutes to allow the flavors to meld together.
11. Garnish with fresh cilantro leaves before serving.
12. Serve hot with rice, naan bread, or roti.

Enjoy your homemade Rajma Masala!

Fish Curry

Ingredients:

- 500g fish fillets (any firm white fish like cod, tilapia, or halibut)
- 2 tablespoons vegetable oil
- 1 onion, finely chopped
- 3 cloves garlic, minced
- 1-inch piece of ginger, grated
- 2 tomatoes, finely chopped or pureed
- 2 green chilies, slit (adjust to taste)
- 1 teaspoon cumin seeds
- 1 teaspoon ground coriander
- 1/2 teaspoon ground turmeric
- 1/2 teaspoon red chili powder (adjust to taste)
- 1/2 teaspoon ground cumin
- 1/2 teaspoon garam masala
- Salt to taste
- 1 cup coconut milk
- Fresh cilantro leaves for garnish
- Lemon wedges for serving (optional)
- Cooked rice or naan bread for serving

Instructions:

1. Heat vegetable oil in a large skillet or pan over medium heat. Add cumin seeds and let them splutter.
2. Add chopped onions to the skillet and sauté until they turn translucent.
3. Add minced garlic and grated ginger to the skillet. Sauté for another minute until fragrant.
4. Add chopped tomatoes or tomato puree to the skillet. Cook until they become soft and mushy.
5. Stir in ground coriander, ground turmeric, red chili powder, ground cumin, and garam masala. Mix well and cook for 2-3 minutes to let the spices toast and release their flavors.
6. Add coconut milk to the skillet and stir until well combined with the spice mixture.

7. Bring the mixture to a gentle simmer and let it cook for 5-7 minutes, allowing the flavors to meld together.
8. Season the fish fillets with salt and gently place them into the simmering curry sauce. Spoon some of the sauce over the fish to coat it.
9. Cover the skillet and let the fish cook in the curry sauce for about 8-10 minutes, or until the fish is cooked through and flakes easily with a fork.
10. Once the fish is cooked, adjust salt and spices according to your taste preferences.
11. Garnish with fresh cilantro leaves before serving.
12. Serve hot with cooked rice or naan bread.
13. Optionally, serve with lemon wedges on the side for squeezing over the fish curry.

Enjoy your homemade Fish Curry!

Pani Puri

Ingredients:

For the Puris:

- 1 cup semolina (sooji/rava)
- 1/4 cup all-purpose flour
- 1/4 teaspoon baking soda
- Salt to taste
- Water, as needed
- Vegetable oil for frying

For the Pani (Spiced Water):

- 1 cup fresh mint leaves
- 1/2 cup fresh coriander leaves
- 2-3 green chilies (adjust to taste)
- 1-inch piece of ginger, chopped
- 1 teaspoon roasted cumin powder
- 1 teaspoon chaat masala
- 1 teaspoon black salt
- 1 teaspoon tamarind paste or pulp
- Salt to taste
- 4 cups cold water

For the Filling:

- 1 cup cooked chickpeas (optional)
- 1 potato, boiled and mashed
- 1 onion, finely chopped
- Tamarind chutney (optional)
- Green chutney (optional)

Instructions:

1. To make the Puris, combine semolina, all-purpose flour, baking soda, and salt in a mixing bowl. Gradually add water and knead into a stiff dough. Cover the dough with a damp cloth and let it rest for 15-20 minutes.
2. Divide the dough into small lemon-sized balls. Roll out each ball into a thin disc, about 2 inches in diameter.
3. Heat vegetable oil in a deep frying pan over medium heat. Once the oil is hot, fry the rolled-out discs until they puff up and turn golden brown. Remove them from the oil using a slotted spoon and drain on paper towels. Repeat the process with the remaining dough.
4. To make the Pani, blend mint leaves, coriander leaves, green chilies, ginger, roasted cumin powder, chaat masala, black salt, tamarind paste/pulp, and salt with cold water in a blender until smooth. Strain the mixture through a fine sieve to remove any solids. Adjust the consistency by adding more water if needed. Refrigerate until ready to use.
5. To assemble the Pani Puri, gently tap the top of each fried puri to create a small hole.
6. Fill each puri with a spoonful of mashed potato and cooked chickpeas (if using). Add chopped onions, tamarind chutney, and green chutney according to your taste preferences.
7. Pour the chilled spiced water (Pani) into each filled puri using a spoon or a small ladle.
8. Serve the Pani Puris immediately and enjoy the burst of flavors!

Enjoy your homemade Pani Puri!

Dum Aloo

Ingredients:

- 500g baby potatoes, peeled
- 2 tablespoons vegetable oil or ghee
- 1 onion, finely chopped
- 2 tomatoes, finely chopped or pureed
- 3 cloves garlic, minced
- 1-inch piece of ginger, grated
- 2 green chilies, slit (adjust to taste)
- 1 teaspoon cumin seeds
- 1 teaspoon ground coriander
- 1/2 teaspoon ground turmeric
- 1/2 teaspoon red chili powder (adjust to taste)
- 1/2 teaspoon garam masala
- Salt to taste
- 1/2 cup plain yogurt
- Fresh cilantro leaves for garnish

Instructions:

1. Boil the baby potatoes until they are fork-tender. Drain the potatoes and let them cool slightly. Prick them with a fork or toothpick.
2. Heat vegetable oil or ghee in a large skillet or pan over medium heat. Add cumin seeds and let them splutter.
3. Add chopped onions to the skillet and sauté until they turn translucent.
4. Add minced garlic, grated ginger, and slit green chilies. Sauté for another 2-3 minutes until fragrant.
5. Add chopped tomatoes or tomato puree to the skillet. Cook until they become soft and mushy.
6. Stir in ground coriander, ground turmeric, red chili powder, and garam masala. Mix well and cook for 2-3 minutes to let the spices toast and release their flavors.
7. Add the boiled baby potatoes to the skillet and mix until they are well coated with the spice mixture.
8. Whisk plain yogurt until smooth and add it to the skillet. Stir until well combined with the potato mixture.

9. Cover the skillet and let the Dum Aloo simmer on low heat for about 15-20 minutes, allowing the flavors to meld together and the potatoes to absorb the sauce, stirring occasionally.
10. Adjust salt and spices according to your taste preferences.
11. Garnish with fresh cilantro leaves before serving.
12. Serve hot with rice or naan bread.

Enjoy your homemade Dum Aloo!

Aloo Paratha

Ingredients:

For the Dough:

- 2 cups whole wheat flour (atta)
- Water, as needed
- Salt to taste

For the Potato Filling:

- 2 large potatoes, boiled, peeled, and mashed
- 1 onion, finely chopped
- 2 green chilies, finely chopped (adjust to taste)
- 1 teaspoon grated ginger
- 1/2 teaspoon cumin seeds
- 1/2 teaspoon ground coriander
- 1/2 teaspoon garam masala
- 1/2 teaspoon red chili powder (adjust to taste)
- Salt to taste
- Fresh cilantro leaves, chopped
- Vegetable oil or ghee for cooking

Instructions:

1. In a large mixing bowl, combine the whole wheat flour and salt. Gradually add water and knead to form a smooth and pliable dough. Cover the dough and let it rest for at least 15-20 minutes.
2. Meanwhile, prepare the potato filling. In a separate bowl, combine the mashed potatoes, chopped onions, chopped green chilies, grated ginger, cumin seeds, ground coriander, garam masala, red chili powder, salt, and chopped cilantro leaves. Mix well until all the ingredients are thoroughly combined.
3. Divide the dough into equal-sized balls and roll each ball into a small disc, about 3-4 inches in diameter.

4. Place a portion of the potato filling in the center of each disc. Bring the edges of the dough together to enclose the filling and pinch to seal.
5. Gently flatten the stuffed dough ball and roll it out into a circle, about 6-7 inches in diameter. Take care not to tear the dough and ensure that the filling is evenly distributed.
6. Heat a tawa or skillet over medium heat. Place the rolled-out paratha on the hot tawa and cook for 1-2 minutes, or until bubbles start to form on the surface.
7. Flip the paratha and brush the cooked side with a little oil or ghee. Cook for another 1-2 minutes, pressing lightly with a spatula until golden brown spots appear on both sides.
8. Repeat the process with the remaining dough balls and potato filling, brushing each side of the paratha with oil or ghee as needed.
9. Serve hot with yogurt, pickle, or your favorite chutney.

Enjoy your homemade Aloo Paratha!

Keema

Ingredients:

- 500g minced meat (beef, lamb, chicken, or turkey)
- 2 tablespoons vegetable oil
- 1 onion, finely chopped
- 3 cloves garlic, minced
- 1-inch piece of ginger, grated
- 2 tomatoes, finely chopped or pureed
- 2 green chilies, chopped (adjust to taste)
- 1 teaspoon cumin seeds
- 1 teaspoon ground coriander
- 1/2 teaspoon ground turmeric
- 1/2 teaspoon red chili powder (adjust to taste)
- 1/2 teaspoon garam masala
- Salt to taste
- Fresh cilantro leaves for garnish

Instructions:

1. Heat vegetable oil in a large skillet or pan over medium heat. Add cumin seeds and let them splutter.
2. Add chopped onions to the skillet and sauté until they turn translucent.
3. Add minced garlic, grated ginger, and chopped green chilies. Sauté for another 2-3 minutes until fragrant.
4. Add chopped tomatoes or tomato puree to the skillet. Cook until they become soft and mushy.
5. Stir in ground coriander, ground turmeric, red chili powder, garam masala, and salt. Mix well and cook for 2-3 minutes to let the spices toast and release their flavors.
6. Add the minced meat to the skillet and mix well with the spice mixture.
7. Cook the keema, stirring occasionally, until the meat is browned and cooked through.
8. Once the keema is cooked, adjust salt and spices according to your taste preferences.
9. Garnish with fresh cilantro leaves before serving.

10. Serve hot with rice, naan bread, or roti.

Enjoy your homemade Keema!

Paneer Butter Masala

Ingredients:

For the Paneer:

- 250g paneer, cut into cubes
- 2 tablespoons vegetable oil or ghee

For the Gravy:

- 2 tablespoons butter
- 1 onion, finely chopped
- 2 tomatoes, finely chopped or pureed
- 3 cloves garlic, minced
- 1-inch piece of ginger, grated
- 2 green chilies, chopped (adjust to taste)
- 1 teaspoon cumin seeds
- 1 teaspoon ground coriander
- 1/2 teaspoon ground turmeric
- 1/2 teaspoon red chili powder (adjust to taste)
- 1/2 teaspoon garam masala
- 1/2 cup cashew nuts, soaked in warm water for 30 minutes and blended into a smooth paste
- 1/4 cup heavy cream
- Salt to taste
- Fresh cilantro leaves for garnish

Instructions:

1. Heat vegetable oil or ghee in a large skillet or pan over medium heat. Add paneer cubes and fry them until golden brown on all sides. Remove the paneer cubes from the skillet and set them aside.
2. In the same skillet, melt butter over medium heat. Add cumin seeds and let them splutter.
3. Add chopped onions to the skillet and sauté until they turn translucent.
4. Add minced garlic, grated ginger, and chopped green chilies. Sauté for another 2-3 minutes until fragrant.

5. Add chopped tomatoes or tomato puree to the skillet. Cook until they become soft and mushy.
6. Stir in ground coriander, ground turmeric, red chili powder, garam masala, and salt. Mix well and cook for 2-3 minutes to let the spices toast and release their flavors.
7. Add the cashew nut paste to the skillet and mix until well combined with the spice mixture. Cook for another 2-3 minutes.
8. Pour in heavy cream and stir until well incorporated. Simmer for 5-7 minutes, stirring occasionally, until the gravy thickens.
9. Add the fried paneer cubes to the skillet and gently mix until they are coated with the gravy. Simmer for another 2-3 minutes to allow the paneer to absorb the flavors of the gravy.
10. Adjust salt according to your taste preferences.
11. Garnish with fresh cilantro leaves before serving.
12. Serve hot with rice, naan bread, or roti.

Enjoy your homemade Paneer Butter Masala!

Chicken 65

Ingredients:

For Marination:

- 500g boneless chicken, cut into bite-sized pieces
- 2 tablespoons yogurt
- 1 tablespoon ginger-garlic paste
- 1 teaspoon red chili powder
- 1/2 teaspoon turmeric powder
- 1 teaspoon garam masala
- 1 teaspoon ground coriander
- 1 teaspoon ground cumin
- 1 tablespoon lemon juice
- Salt to taste

For Coating:

- 3 tablespoons corn flour
- 3 tablespoons all-purpose flour (maida)
- 1 tablespoon rice flour
- Salt to taste
- 1/2 teaspoon red chili powder
- 1/2 teaspoon garam masala
- 1/2 teaspoon ground black pepper

For Frying:

- Vegetable oil for deep frying

For Seasoning:

- 2 tablespoons vegetable oil

- 10-12 curry leaves
- 3-4 green chilies, slit
- 2 cloves garlic, minced
- 1-inch piece of ginger, grated
- 1 onion, thinly sliced
- 1 teaspoon red chili powder (adjust to taste)
- 1 teaspoon garam masala
- 1 teaspoon ground black pepper
- Salt to taste
- Fresh cilantro leaves for garnish
- Lemon wedges for serving

Instructions:

1. In a mixing bowl, combine the boneless chicken pieces with yogurt, ginger-garlic paste, red chili powder, turmeric powder, garam masala, ground coriander, ground cumin, lemon juice, and salt. Mix well to coat the chicken pieces evenly. Marinate for at least 1-2 hours, preferably overnight in the refrigerator.
2. In a separate bowl, mix together corn flour, all-purpose flour, rice flour, salt, red chili powder, garam masala, and ground black pepper. Toss the marinated chicken pieces in this mixture until they are evenly coated.
3. Heat vegetable oil in a deep frying pan or kadhai over medium-high heat. Once the oil is hot, add the coated chicken pieces in batches and fry until they are golden brown and crispy. Remove the fried chicken pieces using a slotted spoon and drain on paper towels to remove excess oil. Repeat the process with the remaining chicken pieces.
4. In a separate skillet or pan, heat vegetable oil over medium heat. Add curry leaves, slit green chilies, minced garlic, and grated ginger. Sauté for a minute until fragrant.
5. Add thinly sliced onions to the skillet and sauté until they turn translucent.
6. Stir in red chili powder, garam masala, ground black pepper, and salt. Mix well.
7. Add the fried chicken pieces to the skillet and toss until they are well coated with the seasoning mixture. Cook for 2-3 minutes, stirring occasionally, to allow the flavors to meld together.
8. Garnish with fresh cilantro leaves before serving.
9. Serve hot with lemon wedges on the side.

Enjoy your delicious Chicken 65!

Vegetable Pakora

Ingredients:

- 1 cup chickpea flour (besan)
- 2 tablespoons rice flour
- 1 teaspoon cumin seeds
- 1 teaspoon coriander seeds, crushed
- 1/2 teaspoon turmeric powder
- 1/2 teaspoon red chili powder (adjust to taste)
- 1/2 teaspoon baking powder
- Salt to taste
- 1 medium onion, thinly sliced
- 1 medium potato, peeled and thinly sliced
- 1 medium carrot, peeled and grated
- 1/2 cup spinach leaves, chopped
- 2-3 green chilies, finely chopped (adjust to taste)
- Handful of fresh cilantro leaves, chopped
- Water, as needed
- Vegetable oil for deep frying

Instructions:

1. In a large mixing bowl, combine chickpea flour, rice flour, cumin seeds, crushed coriander seeds, turmeric powder, red chili powder, baking powder, and salt. Mix well.
2. Add thinly sliced onions, thinly sliced potatoes, grated carrots, chopped spinach leaves, chopped green chilies, and chopped cilantro leaves to the dry ingredients. Mix until the vegetables are evenly coated with the flour mixture.
3. Gradually add water, a little at a time, and mix until you have a thick batter consistency. The batter should coat the vegetables well.
4. Heat vegetable oil in a deep frying pan or kadhai over medium-high heat.
5. Once the oil is hot, drop spoonfuls of the vegetable batter into the hot oil, making sure not to overcrowd the pan.
6. Fry the pakoras in batches until they are golden brown and crispy, about 3-4 minutes per batch. Use a slotted spoon to remove the pakoras from the oil and drain them on paper towels to remove excess oil.
7. Repeat the process with the remaining batter, frying the pakoras in batches.

8. Serve the vegetable pakoras hot with mint chutney, tamarind chutney, or tomato ketchup.

Enjoy your homemade Vegetable Pakoras as a delicious snack or appetizer!

Dosa

Ingredients:

For Dosa Batter:

- 1 cup rice (preferably parboiled rice or idli rice)
- 1/4 cup urad dal (split black gram)
- 1/2 teaspoon fenugreek seeds (methi seeds)
- Water, as needed
- Salt to taste

For Making Dosas:

- Vegetable oil or ghee, for cooking dosas
- Dosa batter (prepared as per instructions above)

Instructions:

1. Rinse the rice, urad dal, and fenugreek seeds separately under cold water. Soak them in water for about 4-6 hours or overnight.
2. After soaking, drain the water from the rice, urad dal, and fenugreek seeds. Transfer them to a blender or wet grinder. Add water gradually and grind them to a smooth batter. The consistency should be similar to pancake batter. Add salt to taste and mix well.
3. Transfer the batter to a large bowl. Cover it with a clean kitchen towel or plastic wrap and let it ferment in a warm place for about 8-12 hours or until it becomes slightly sour and doubles in volume.
4. Once the batter is fermented, gently stir it to mix well.
5. Heat a non-stick or cast-iron dosa tawa (griddle) over medium-high heat. Once the tawa is hot, sprinkle a few drops of water on it. If the water sizzles and evaporates immediately, the tawa is ready for making dosas.
6. Reduce the heat to medium-low. Pour a ladleful of dosa batter onto the center of the tawa. Using the back of the ladle, spread the batter in a circular motion to form a thin, even layer. You can make the dosa as thin or thick as you prefer.

7. Drizzle a little vegetable oil or ghee around the edges of the dosa. Let it cook until the edges start to lift off the tawa and turn golden brown.
8. Carefully flip the dosa using a spatula. Cook the other side for another minute or until it turns golden brown and crispy.
9. Remove the dosa from the tawa and transfer it to a serving plate.
10. Repeat the process with the remaining batter, making more dosas as needed.
11. Serve the dosas hot with coconut chutney, sambar, or any other side dish of your choice.

Enjoy your homemade dosas!

Raita

Ingredients:

- 1 cup plain yogurt
- 1/2 cucumber, grated or finely chopped
- 1 medium tomato, finely chopped
- 1/4 cup red onion, finely chopped (optional)
- 1-2 green chilies, finely chopped (adjust to taste)
- 1 tablespoon fresh cilantro leaves, chopped
- 1/2 teaspoon roasted cumin powder
- Salt to taste
- Pinch of black salt (optional)
- Pinch of red chili powder (optional)
- Fresh mint leaves for garnish (optional)

Instructions:

1. In a mixing bowl, whisk the plain yogurt until smooth.
2. Add grated or finely chopped cucumber, chopped tomato, chopped red onion (if using), chopped green chilies, and chopped cilantro leaves to the yogurt. Mix well to combine.
3. Season the raita with roasted cumin powder, salt, black salt (if using), and red chili powder (if using). Adjust the seasoning according to your taste preferences.
4. Garnish the raita with fresh mint leaves (if using).
5. Cover the bowl and refrigerate the raita for at least 30 minutes to allow the flavors to meld together.
6. Before serving, give the raita a quick stir and adjust the consistency by adding a little water if it's too thick.
7. Serve the chilled raita as a refreshing side dish with biryani, pulao, kebabs, or any other Indian main course.

Enjoy your homemade raita!

Gajar Ka Halwa

Ingredients:

- 500g carrots, grated
- 2 cups full-fat milk
- 4 tablespoons ghee (clarified butter)
- 1/2 cup sugar (adjust to taste)
- 1/4 cup khoya (mawa), crumbled (optional)
- 1/4 cup chopped nuts (cashews, almonds, pistachios, etc.)
- 1/2 teaspoon cardamom powder
- Saffron strands (optional)
- Raisins for garnish (optional)

Instructions:

1. Rinse, peel, and grate the carrots using a grater or food processor. Set aside.
2. Heat 2 tablespoons of ghee in a heavy-bottomed pan or kadhai over medium heat. Add the grated carrots and sauté for 5-7 minutes, stirring frequently.
3. Pour in the milk and stir well to combine with the carrots. Bring the mixture to a simmer.
4. Cook the carrot mixture on low heat, stirring occasionally, until the carrots are cooked and the milk is reduced to about half its original volume. This may take about 30-40 minutes.
5. Add sugar to the carrot mixture and stir well until the sugar is dissolved. Cook for another 10-15 minutes, stirring frequently, until the mixture thickens.
6. If using khoya, crumble it and add it to the halwa. Stir well until the khoya is fully incorporated into the mixture.
7. In a separate small pan, heat the remaining 2 tablespoons of ghee. Add the chopped nuts and sauté until they turn golden brown. Add the sautéed nuts to the halwa mixture along with cardamom powder and mix well.
8. Optionally, you can add saffron strands soaked in a little warm milk for added flavor and color.
9. Cook the halwa for another 5-10 minutes, stirring continuously, until it reaches a thick and pudding-like consistency.
10. Remove the pan from the heat. Garnish the Gajar ka Halwa with raisins and additional chopped nuts if desired.

11. Serve the Gajar ka Halwa warm or cold. It can be enjoyed on its own or with a scoop of vanilla ice cream for a delightful treat.

Enjoy your homemade Gajar ka Halwa!

Chicken Biryani

Ingredients:

For Marinating Chicken:

- 500g chicken, cut into pieces
- 1 cup yogurt
- 2 tablespoons ginger-garlic paste
- 1 teaspoon red chili powder
- 1/2 teaspoon turmeric powder
- 1 teaspoon garam masala
- Salt to taste

For Biryani Masala:

- 2 tablespoons vegetable oil or ghee
- 2 onions, thinly sliced
- 2 tomatoes, finely chopped
- 2 green chilies, slit (adjust to taste)
- 1 tablespoon ginger-garlic paste
- 1 teaspoon red chili powder
- 1/2 teaspoon turmeric powder
- 1 teaspoon ground coriander
- 1 teaspoon ground cumin
- 1/2 teaspoon ground cardamom
- 1/2 teaspoon ground cinnamon
- 1/2 teaspoon ground cloves
- 1/2 teaspoon ground black pepper
- Salt to taste
- Handful of fresh cilantro leaves, chopped
- Handful of fresh mint leaves, chopped

For Rice:

- 2 cups Basmati rice, soaked in water for 30 minutes and drained

- 4 cups water
- 1 bay leaf
- 2-3 cloves
- 2-3 green cardamom pods
- Salt to taste

For Layering:

- Saffron strands soaked in warm milk
- Fried onions (optional)
- Ghee for drizzling

Instructions:

1. Marinate the chicken pieces with yogurt, ginger-garlic paste, red chili powder, turmeric powder, garam masala, and salt. Cover and refrigerate for at least 1 hour.
2. Heat vegetable oil or ghee in a large skillet or pan over medium heat. Add sliced onions and sauté until golden brown. Remove half of the fried onions and set them aside for layering.
3. To the remaining onions in the pan, add chopped tomatoes, slit green chilies, and ginger-garlic paste. Cook until the tomatoes turn soft and mushy.
4. Add red chili powder, turmeric powder, ground coriander, ground cumin, ground cardamom, ground cinnamon, ground cloves, ground black pepper, and salt to the pan. Mix well and cook for a couple of minutes until the spices are fragrant.
5. Add marinated chicken pieces to the pan along with chopped cilantro leaves and mint leaves. Cook for 5-7 minutes until the chicken is partially cooked. Remove from heat and set aside.
6. In a large pot, bring water to a boil. Add soaked and drained Basmati rice, bay leaf, cloves, green cardamom pods, and salt. Cook the rice until it's about 70-80% cooked. Drain the rice and set aside.
7. Preheat the oven to 350°F (180°C).
8. To assemble the biryani, spread a layer of cooked rice at the bottom of a large oven-safe dish. Top it with a layer of the partially cooked chicken masala. Repeat the layers until all the rice and chicken masala are used up.
9. Drizzle saffron milk over the top layer of rice. Sprinkle the reserved fried onions over the rice.

10. Cover the dish with aluminum foil and bake in the preheated oven for 20-25 minutes, or until the chicken is fully cooked and the flavors are well combined.
11. Remove the biryani from the oven and let it rest for a few minutes before serving.
12. Serve the Chicken Biryani hot with raita, salad, or your favorite side dish.

Enjoy your homemade Chicken Biryani!

Veg Pulao

Ingredients:

- 1 cup Basmati rice, soaked in water for 30 minutes and drained
- 2 tablespoons ghee or vegetable oil
- 1 onion, thinly sliced
- 1 carrot, diced
- 1 potato, diced
- 1/2 cup green peas (fresh or frozen)
- 1/2 cup cauliflower florets
- 1/2 cup green beans, chopped
- 2 green chilies, slit (adjust to taste)
- 1-inch piece of ginger, grated
- 2 cloves garlic, minced
- 2 cups water or vegetable broth
- 1 bay leaf
- 2-3 cloves
- 2-3 green cardamom pods
- 1-inch cinnamon stick
- Salt to taste
- Fresh cilantro leaves for garnish
- Lemon wedges for serving (optional)

Instructions:

1. Heat ghee or vegetable oil in a large pot or pressure cooker over medium heat.
2. Add sliced onions and sauté until they turn golden brown.
3. Add grated ginger, minced garlic, and slit green chilies. Sauté for another minute until fragrant.
4. Add diced carrots, potatoes, green peas, cauliflower florets, and chopped green beans to the pot. Stir well to combine with the onions and spices.
5. Drain the soaked Basmati rice and add it to the pot. Sauté for 2-3 minutes, stirring gently to coat the rice with the vegetables and spices.
6. Pour water or vegetable broth into the pot. Add bay leaf, cloves, green cardamom pods, cinnamon stick, and salt to taste. Mix well.

7. Bring the mixture to a boil. If using a pressure cooker, cover with the lid and cook on medium heat for 1 whistle. If using a regular pot, cover with a lid and cook until the rice is tender and the water is absorbed, about 15-20 minutes.
8. Once the pulao is cooked, remove it from heat and let it sit covered for 5-10 minutes.
9. Fluff the pulao gently with a fork to separate the grains.
10. Garnish with fresh cilantro leaves before serving. Serve hot with lemon wedges on the side if desired.

Enjoy your homemade Vegetable Pulao as a delicious and nutritious meal!

Rasgulla

Ingredients:

For Rasgulla Balls:

- 1 liter (4 cups) full-fat milk
- 2 tablespoons lemon juice or white vinegar
- 2 cups sugar
- 4 cups water
- 2-3 green cardamom pods, lightly crushed (optional)
- A few saffron strands (optional)
- Rose water or kewra water (optional)

Instructions:

1. In a large pot, bring the milk to a boil over medium heat, stirring occasionally to prevent burning.
2. Once the milk comes to a boil, reduce the heat to low. Add lemon juice or white vinegar gradually, stirring continuously, until the milk curdles and separates into curds (chenna) and whey (greenish liquid).
3. Turn off the heat and let the mixture sit for a few minutes to allow the curds to fully separate from the whey.
4. Line a large strainer or colander with a cheesecloth or muslin cloth. Place it over a bowl to collect the whey. Carefully pour the curdled milk into the strainer.
5. Rinse the chenna under cold water to remove any traces of lemon juice or vinegar. Gather the edges of the cloth and squeeze gently to remove excess water.
6. Hang the cloth with the chenna for about 30 minutes to drain any remaining water.
7. After draining, transfer the chenna to a clean, dry surface. Knead the chenna with the heel of your hand for about 5-7 minutes until it becomes smooth and soft.
8. Divide the chenna into small equal-sized portions and roll them into smooth balls between your palms. Make sure there are no cracks on the surface of the balls.
9. In a separate pot, combine sugar and water. Bring it to a boil over medium heat, stirring occasionally to dissolve the sugar completely.

10. Once the sugar syrup comes to a boil, reduce the heat to low. Gently add the rasgulla balls to the syrup one by one.
11. Cover the pot with a lid and let the rasgullas simmer in the syrup for about 15-20 minutes. During this time, the rasgullas will double in size and become spongy.
12. If using, add crushed cardamom pods, saffron strands, and a few drops of rose water or kewra water to the syrup for flavoring.
13. Turn off the heat and let the rasgullas cool down in the syrup for at least 1-2 hours.
14. Once cooled, transfer the rasgullas along with the syrup to a serving dish.
15. Serve the rasgullas chilled or at room temperature. Enjoy this delicious Indian sweet as a dessert!

Note: Rasgullas can be stored in the refrigerator for up to 3-4 days.

Aloo Tikki

Ingredients:

- 4 medium potatoes, boiled, peeled, and mashed
- 1/2 cup bread crumbs
- 1/4 cup finely chopped onions
- 1/4 cup finely chopped cilantro leaves
- 2 green chilies, finely chopped (adjust to taste)
- 1 teaspoon ginger-garlic paste
- 1/2 teaspoon garam masala
- 1/2 teaspoon ground cumin
- 1/2 teaspoon ground coriander
- 1/2 teaspoon red chili powder (adjust to taste)
- Salt to taste
- Vegetable oil for shallow frying

Instructions:

1. In a large mixing bowl, combine the mashed potatoes, bread crumbs, chopped onions, chopped cilantro leaves, chopped green chilies, ginger-garlic paste, garam masala, ground cumin, ground coriander, red chili powder, and salt. Mix well to combine all the ingredients.
2. Divide the mixture into equal-sized portions and shape each portion into round or oval patties.
3. Heat vegetable oil in a skillet or frying pan over medium heat.
4. Once the oil is hot, carefully place the aloo tikkis in the pan, leaving enough space between them. You may need to fry them in batches depending on the size of your pan.
5. Shallow fry the aloo tikkis until they are golden brown and crispy on both sides, flipping them occasionally to ensure even cooking.
6. Once done, remove the aloo tikkis from the pan and drain them on paper towels to remove excess oil.
7. Serve the aloo tikkis hot with mint chutney, tamarind chutney, or tomato ketchup. You can also serve them with yogurt and chaat masala for a delicious twist.
8. Enjoy your homemade aloo tikkis as a tasty snack or appetizer!

You can also experiment with stuffing the aloo tikkis with paneer, cheese, or a spicy mixture for extra flavor.

Mutton Curry

Ingredients:

- 500g mutton, cut into pieces
- 3 tablespoons vegetable oil
- 2 onions, finely chopped
- 3 tomatoes, finely chopped or pureed
- 2 green chilies, slit (adjust to taste)
- 1 tablespoon ginger-garlic paste
- 1 teaspoon red chili powder (adjust to taste)
- 1/2 teaspoon turmeric powder
- 1 teaspoon ground coriander
- 1 teaspoon ground cumin
- 1/2 teaspoon garam masala
- Salt to taste
- Fresh cilantro leaves for garnish

Instructions:

1. Heat vegetable oil in a large skillet or pressure cooker over medium heat.
2. Add finely chopped onions to the skillet and sauté until they turn golden brown.
3. Add ginger-garlic paste and slit green chilies. Sauté for another 2-3 minutes until fragrant.
4. Add chopped or pureed tomatoes to the skillet. Cook until they become soft and mushy.
5. Stir in red chili powder, turmeric powder, ground coriander, ground cumin, garam masala, and salt. Mix well and cook for 2-3 minutes to let the spices toast and release their flavors.
6. Add the mutton pieces to the skillet and mix well with the spice mixture. Cook for 5-7 minutes until the mutton is browned.
7. If using a pressure cooker, add water as needed to cover the mutton pieces. Close the lid and cook on medium heat for about 5-6 whistles or until the mutton is tender.
8. If using a skillet, add water as needed to cover the mutton pieces. Cover the skillet with a lid and cook on low heat for about 45-60 minutes or until the mutton is tender, stirring occasionally and adding more water if needed.

9. Once the mutton is cooked and tender, check for seasoning and adjust salt and spices according to your taste preferences.
10. Garnish the mutton curry with fresh cilantro leaves before serving.
11. Serve hot with rice, naan bread, or roti.

Enjoy your homemade Mutton Curry!

Papdi Chaat

Ingredients:

For Papdi:

- 1 cup all-purpose flour (maida)
- 1/4 teaspoon ajwain (carom seeds)
- 1/4 teaspoon salt
- 1 tablespoon vegetable oil
- Water, as needed
- Vegetable oil for deep frying

For Assembling Chaat:

- 1 cup boiled chickpeas (or canned chickpeas, drained and rinsed)
- 1 cup boiled potatoes, diced
- 1/2 cup chopped onions
- 1/2 cup chopped tomatoes
- 1/4 cup chopped cilantro leaves
- 1/4 cup tamarind chutney
- 1/4 cup mint chutney
- 1/4 cup plain yogurt (optional)
- Chaat masala, to taste
- Red chili powder, to taste
- Roasted cumin powder, to taste
- Sev (crispy chickpea flour noodles)
- Fresh cilantro leaves for garnish

Instructions:

For Papdi:

1. In a mixing bowl, combine all-purpose flour, ajwain, salt, and vegetable oil. Mix well.

2. Gradually add water, a little at a time, and knead the mixture into a stiff dough.
3. Divide the dough into small lemon-sized portions. Roll out each portion into a thin disc using a rolling pin.
4. Prick the rolled-out dough with a fork to prevent puffing during frying.
5. Heat vegetable oil in a deep frying pan or kadhai over medium heat. Once the oil is hot, fry the rolled-out discs until golden brown and crispy. Remove them from the oil and drain on paper towels to remove excess oil. Let them cool.

For Assembling Chaat:

1. Arrange the fried papdis on a serving plate.
2. Top each papdi with boiled chickpeas, diced boiled potatoes, chopped onions, and chopped tomatoes.
3. Drizzle tamarind chutney and mint chutney over the assembled papdis.
4. If using yogurt, drizzle it over the papdis as well.
5. Sprinkle chaat masala, red chili powder, and roasted cumin powder over the papdis according to your taste preferences.
6. Garnish with sev and fresh cilantro leaves.
7. Serve the Papdi Chaat immediately as a delicious and flavorful snack or appetizer.

Enjoy your homemade Papdi Chaat!

Chicken Chettinad

Ingredients:

- 500g chicken, cut into pieces
- 2 onions, finely chopped
- 2 tomatoes, finely chopped
- 3-4 green chilies, slit (adjust to taste)
- 10-12 curry leaves
- 1-inch piece of ginger, grated
- 5-6 garlic cloves, minced
- 1/2 cup grated coconut (fresh or desiccated)
- 2 tablespoons vegetable oil
- 1 teaspoon mustard seeds
- 1 teaspoon cumin seeds
- 1 teaspoon fennel seeds
- 1 teaspoon whole black peppercorns
- 2-3 dried red chilies
- 2 teaspoons coriander seeds
- 1 teaspoon cumin seeds
- 1/2 teaspoon turmeric powder
- 1 tablespoon red chili powder (adjust to taste)
- 1 tablespoon ground coriander
- 1/2 teaspoon garam masala
- Salt to taste
- Fresh cilantro leaves for garnish

Instructions:

1. Dry roast grated coconut in a pan over medium heat until it turns golden brown. Remove from heat and set aside.
2. Dry roast mustard seeds, cumin seeds, fennel seeds, whole black peppercorns, dried red chilies, coriander seeds, and cumin seeds until fragrant. Allow them to cool down, then grind them into a fine powder using a spice grinder or mortar and pestle. Set aside.
3. Heat vegetable oil in a large skillet or pan over medium heat. Add chopped onions and sauté until they turn golden brown.

4. Add grated ginger, minced garlic, slit green chilies, and curry leaves to the skillet. Sauté for another 2-3 minutes until fragrant.
5. Add chopped tomatoes to the skillet and cook until they become soft and mushy.
6. Stir in turmeric powder, red chili powder, ground coriander, and the ground spice powder mixture. Mix well and cook for 2-3 minutes to let the spices toast and release their flavors.
7. Add the chicken pieces to the skillet and mix well with the spice mixture. Cook for 5-7 minutes until the chicken is browned.
8. Add the roasted grated coconut to the skillet and mix well with the chicken and spices.
9. Pour in water as needed to cover the chicken pieces. Bring the mixture to a simmer, then cover and cook for about 20-25 minutes or until the chicken is cooked through and tender.
10. Once the chicken is cooked, sprinkle garam masala and salt to taste. Mix well and simmer for another 5 minutes.
11. Garnish with fresh cilantro leaves before serving.
12. Serve hot with steamed rice, roti, or naan bread.

Enjoy your homemade Chicken Chettinad!

Gobi Manchurian

Ingredients:

For Cauliflower Fritters (Gobi):

- 1 medium cauliflower, cut into small florets
- 1/2 cup all-purpose flour (maida)
- 1/4 cup cornstarch
- 1 teaspoon ginger-garlic paste
- 1 teaspoon soy sauce
- 1/2 teaspoon red chili powder (adjust to taste)
- Salt to taste
- Water, as needed
- Vegetable oil for deep frying

For Manchurian Sauce:

- 2 tablespoons vegetable oil
- 3-4 cloves garlic, minced
- 1-inch piece of ginger, grated
- 2 green chilies, finely chopped
- 1 onion, finely chopped
- 1 bell pepper (capsicum), finely chopped
- 2 tablespoons soy sauce
- 1 tablespoon chili sauce (adjust to taste)
- 1 tablespoon tomato ketchup
- 1 tablespoon vinegar
- 1 teaspoon sugar
- 1 teaspoon cornstarch mixed with 2 tablespoons water (cornstarch slurry)
- Salt to taste
- Fresh cilantro leaves for garnish

Instructions:

For Cauliflower Fritters (Gobi):

1. In a large mixing bowl, combine all-purpose flour, cornstarch, ginger-garlic paste, soy sauce, red chili powder, and salt. Mix well.
2. Gradually add water, a little at a time, and whisk until you have a smooth batter with a thick consistency.
3. Dip each cauliflower floret into the batter, making sure it is well coated.
4. Heat vegetable oil in a deep frying pan or kadhai over medium heat. Once the oil is hot, carefully add the battered cauliflower florets in batches and fry until they are golden brown and crispy. Remove them from the oil using a slotted spoon and drain on paper towels to remove excess oil. Set aside.

For Manchurian Sauce:

1. Heat vegetable oil in a large skillet or wok over medium-high heat.
2. Add minced garlic, grated ginger, and chopped green chilies to the skillet. Sauté for a minute until fragrant.
3. Add finely chopped onions and bell peppers (capsicum) to the skillet. Stir-fry for 2-3 minutes until they become tender-crisp.
4. Stir in soy sauce, chili sauce, tomato ketchup, vinegar, sugar, and salt. Mix well to combine all the ingredients.
5. Add the cornstarch slurry to the skillet and stir continuously until the sauce thickens slightly.
6. Add the fried cauliflower florets to the skillet and toss well to coat them evenly with the sauce.
7. Cook for another 2-3 minutes, stirring occasionally, until the cauliflower is heated through and the sauce coats the florets nicely.
8. Garnish with fresh cilantro leaves before serving.
9. Serve hot as an appetizer or as a side dish with fried rice or noodles.

Enjoy your homemade Gobi Manchurian!

Mutton Biryani

Ingredients:

For Marinating Mutton:

- 500g mutton, cut into pieces
- 1 cup yogurt
- 2 tablespoons ginger-garlic paste
- 1 teaspoon red chili powder
- 1/2 teaspoon turmeric powder
- 1 teaspoon garam masala
- Salt to taste

For Biryani Rice:

- 2 cups Basmati rice, soaked in water for 30 minutes and drained
- 4 cups water
- 1 bay leaf
- 2-3 cloves
- 2-3 green cardamom pods
- Salt to taste

For Biryani Masala:

- 2 tablespoons ghee or vegetable oil
- 2 onions, thinly sliced
- 2 tomatoes, finely chopped
- 2 green chilies, slit (adjust to taste)
- 1 tablespoon ginger-garlic paste
- 1 teaspoon red chili powder
- 1/2 teaspoon turmeric powder
- 1 teaspoon ground coriander
- 1 teaspoon ground cumin
- 1/2 teaspoon ground cardamom
- 1/2 teaspoon ground cinnamon

- 1/2 teaspoon ground cloves
- 1/2 teaspoon ground black pepper
- Salt to taste
- Handful of fresh cilantro leaves, chopped
- Handful of fresh mint leaves, chopped

For Layering:

- Saffron strands soaked in warm milk
- Fried onions (optional)
- Ghee for drizzling

Instructions:

1. Marinate the mutton pieces with yogurt, ginger-garlic paste, red chili powder, turmeric powder, garam masala, and salt. Cover and refrigerate for at least 1 hour.
2. In a large pot, bring water to a boil. Add soaked and drained Basmati rice, bay leaf, cloves, green cardamom pods, and salt. Cook the rice until it's about 70-80% cooked. Drain the rice and set aside.
3. Heat ghee or vegetable oil in a large skillet or pan over medium heat. Add sliced onions and sauté until they turn golden brown.
4. To the skillet, add chopped tomatoes, slit green chilies, and ginger-garlic paste. Cook until the tomatoes turn soft and mushy.
5. Add red chili powder, turmeric powder, ground coriander, ground cumin, ground cardamom, ground cinnamon, ground cloves, ground black pepper, and salt to the skillet. Mix well and cook for a couple of minutes until the spices are fragrant.
6. Add the marinated mutton pieces to the skillet along with chopped cilantro leaves and mint leaves. Cook for 5-7 minutes until the mutton is partially cooked.
7. Preheat the oven to 350°F (180°C).
8. To assemble the biryani, spread a layer of cooked rice at the bottom of a large oven-safe dish. Top it with a layer of the partially cooked mutton masala. Repeat the layers until all the rice and mutton masala are used up.
9. Drizzle saffron milk over the top layer of rice. Sprinkle the fried onions over the rice.
10. Cover the dish with aluminum foil and bake in the preheated oven for 20-25 minutes, or until the mutton is fully cooked and the flavors are well combined.

11. Remove the biryani from the oven and let it rest for a few minutes before serving.
12. Serve the Mutton Biryani hot with raita, salad, or your favorite side dish.

Enjoy your homemade Mutton Biryani!

Chicken Saag

Ingredients:

- 500g boneless chicken, cut into bite-sized pieces
- 500g fresh spinach leaves, washed and chopped
- 1 onion, finely chopped
- 2 tomatoes, finely chopped
- 3-4 garlic cloves, minced
- 1-inch piece of ginger, grated
- 2 green chilies, chopped (adjust to taste)
- 1 teaspoon cumin seeds
- 1 teaspoon ground coriander
- 1/2 teaspoon turmeric powder
- 1/2 teaspoon red chili powder (adjust to taste)
- 1/2 teaspoon garam masala
- Salt to taste
- 2 tablespoons vegetable oil or ghee
- 1/4 cup heavy cream (optional)
- Fresh cilantro leaves for garnish

Instructions:

1. Heat vegetable oil or ghee in a large skillet or pan over medium heat. Add cumin seeds and let them splutter.
2. Add finely chopped onion to the skillet and sauté until it turns golden brown.
3. Add minced garlic, grated ginger, and chopped green chilies to the skillet. Sauté for another 2-3 minutes until fragrant.
4. Add chopped tomatoes to the skillet and cook until they become soft and mushy.
5. Stir in ground coriander, turmeric powder, red chili powder, and salt. Mix well and cook for 2-3 minutes to let the spices toast and release their flavors.
6. Add chopped spinach leaves to the skillet and mix well with the spice mixture. Cook until the spinach wilts down and becomes tender.
7. Once the spinach is cooked, remove the skillet from heat and let the mixture cool down slightly.

8. Transfer the spinach mixture to a blender or food processor and blend it into a smooth puree. You can add a little water if needed to achieve the desired consistency.
9. Return the pureed spinach mixture to the skillet. Add chicken pieces to the skillet and mix well with the spinach sauce.
10. Cover the skillet and let the chicken cook in the spinach sauce over medium-low heat for about 15-20 minutes, or until the chicken is cooked through and tender.
11. Stir in garam masala and heavy cream (if using) to the skillet. Mix well and simmer for another 2-3 minutes.
12. Garnish with fresh cilantro leaves before serving.
13. Serve the Chicken Saag hot with rice, naan bread, or roti.

Enjoy your homemade Chicken Saag!

Egg Curry

Ingredients:

- 6 eggs, hard-boiled, peeled, and halved
- 2 onions, finely chopped
- 2 tomatoes, finely chopped
- 3-4 garlic cloves, minced
- 1-inch piece of ginger, grated
- 2 green chilies, slit (adjust to taste)
- 1 teaspoon cumin seeds
- 1 teaspoon ground coriander
- 1/2 teaspoon turmeric powder
- 1 teaspoon red chili powder (adjust to taste)
- 1/2 teaspoon garam masala
- Salt to taste
- 2 tablespoons vegetable oil or ghee
- Handful of fresh cilantro leaves for garnish

Instructions:

1. Heat vegetable oil or ghee in a large skillet or pan over medium heat. Add cumin seeds and let them splutter.
2. Add finely chopped onion to the skillet and sauté until it turns golden brown.
3. Add minced garlic, grated ginger, and slit green chilies to the skillet. Sauté for another 2-3 minutes until fragrant.
4. Add chopped tomatoes to the skillet and cook until they become soft and mushy.
5. Stir in ground coriander, turmeric powder, red chili powder, and salt. Mix well and cook for 2-3 minutes to let the spices toast and release their flavors.
6. Add about 1-1.5 cups of water to the skillet to create the gravy. Bring the mixture to a simmer.
7. Carefully add the halved boiled eggs to the skillet, making sure they are submerged in the gravy.
8. Cover the skillet and let the eggs simmer in the gravy over medium-low heat for about 10-15 minutes, allowing the flavors to blend and the eggs to absorb the spices.

9. Once the gravy has thickened to your desired consistency and the eggs are heated through, sprinkle garam masala over the curry and mix gently.
10. Garnish with fresh cilantro leaves before serving.
11. Serve the Egg Curry hot with rice, naan bread, or roti.

Enjoy your homemade Egg Curry!

Hyderabadi Biryani

Ingredients:

For Marinating the Chicken:

- 1 kg chicken, cut into pieces
- 1 cup yogurt
- 2 tablespoons ginger-garlic paste
- 2 green chilies, slit lengthwise
- 1 teaspoon red chili powder
- 1/2 teaspoon turmeric powder
- 1 teaspoon garam masala
- Salt to taste

For Rice:

- 2 cups Basmati rice, soaked in water for 30 minutes and drained
- 4 cups water
- 1 bay leaf
- 2-3 cloves
- 2-3 green cardamom pods
- Salt to taste

For Biryani Masala:

- 3 onions, thinly sliced
- 3 tomatoes, chopped
- 2 green chilies, chopped
- 1/4 cup chopped mint leaves
- 1/4 cup chopped cilantro leaves
- 1/4 cup fried onions (for garnish)
- 1/2 cup ghee or vegetable oil
- 1/2 teaspoon saffron strands, soaked in 2 tablespoons warm milk
- 1/4 cup rose water (optional)
- Salt to taste

For Layering:

- Fried onions
- Chopped mint leaves
- Chopped cilantro leaves
- Saffron milk
- Ghee

Instructions:

1. Marinate the chicken pieces with yogurt, ginger-garlic paste, green chilies, red chili powder, turmeric powder, garam masala, and salt. Cover and refrigerate for at least 2 hours.
2. In a large pot, bring water to a boil. Add soaked and drained Basmati rice, bay leaf, cloves, green cardamom pods, and salt. Cook the rice until it's about 70-80% cooked. Drain the rice and set aside.
3. In a separate pan, heat ghee or vegetable oil over medium heat. Add thinly sliced onions and sauté until they turn golden brown.
4. Add chopped tomatoes and green chilies to the pan. Cook until the tomatoes become soft and mushy.
5. Stir in chopped mint leaves and cilantro leaves. Cook for another minute.
6. Add marinated chicken pieces to the pan along with any marinade left in the bowl. Mix well and cook for 10-15 minutes until the chicken is partially cooked and the masala is fragrant.
7. In a large heavy-bottomed pot or Dutch oven, layer half of the partially cooked rice at the bottom. Top it with half of the chicken masala.
8. Sprinkle some fried onions, chopped mint leaves, and chopped cilantro leaves over the chicken masala.
9. Layer the remaining rice over the chicken masala, followed by the remaining chicken masala.
10. Sprinkle the remaining fried onions, chopped mint leaves, and chopped cilantro leaves over the top.
11. Drizzle saffron milk and rose water (if using) over the layered biryani.
12. Dot the top with ghee.
13. Cover the pot tightly with a lid or aluminum foil to seal in the steam.
14. Place the pot on a tava (griddle) or a hot pan and cook on low heat for about 30-40 minutes, or until the chicken is fully cooked and the rice is tender.

15. Once done, gently mix the layers before serving.
16. Serve the Hyderabadi Biryani hot with raita, salad, or your favorite side dish.

Enjoy the rich and aromatic flavors of Hyderabadi Biryani!

Rasam

Ingredients:

- 2 ripe tomatoes, chopped
- 1 tablespoon tamarind paste
- 1 teaspoon mustard seeds
- 1 teaspoon cumin seeds
- 1/2 teaspoon fenugreek seeds
- 2-3 dried red chilies
- 8-10 curry leaves
- 1 teaspoon turmeric powder
- 1 teaspoon rasam powder (or sambar powder)
- 1 tablespoon chopped cilantro leaves
- Salt to taste
- Water
- 1 tablespoon ghee or vegetable oil

Instructions:

1. In a bowl, soak tamarind paste in 1 cup of warm water for about 10 minutes. Then, strain the tamarind water and set it aside.
2. In a pan, heat ghee or vegetable oil over medium heat. Add mustard seeds, cumin seeds, fenugreek seeds, dried red chilies, and curry leaves. Let them splutter and release their aroma.
3. Add chopped tomatoes to the pan along with turmeric powder and salt. Cook until the tomatoes become soft and mushy.
4. Add the strained tamarind water to the pan and bring it to a boil. Let it simmer for a few minutes until the raw smell of tamarind disappears.
5. Add rasam powder (or sambar powder) to the pan and mix well. Adjust the consistency by adding water if needed.
6. Let the rasam simmer for a couple of minutes, allowing the flavors to meld together.
7. Garnish with chopped cilantro leaves and turn off the heat.
8. Serve hot rasam as a soup or with steamed rice and your favorite side dishes.

Enjoy the comforting and flavorful Tomato Rasam! You can adjust the spiciness and tanginess according to your taste preferences.

Gulab Jamun

Ingredients:

For Gulab Jamun:

- 1 cup milk powder
- 1/4 cup all-purpose flour
- 1/4 teaspoon baking soda
- 2 tablespoons ghee or unsalted butter, melted
- 2-3 tablespoons milk (as needed to knead the dough)
- Vegetable oil for frying

For Sugar Syrup (Chashni):

- 1 cup sugar
- 1 cup water
- 2-3 green cardamom pods, lightly crushed
- A few saffron strands (optional)
- 1 teaspoon rose water or kewra water (optional)

Instructions:

1. In a mixing bowl, combine milk powder, all-purpose flour, and baking soda. Mix well.
2. Add melted ghee or unsalted butter to the dry ingredients. Mix until the mixture resembles breadcrumbs.
3. Gradually add milk, a little at a time, and knead the mixture into a soft, smooth dough. The dough should be soft but not sticky. If it's too dry, add a little more milk.
4. Divide the dough into small equal-sized portions and roll them into smooth, crack-free balls between your palms. Make sure there are no cracks on the surface of the balls.
5. Heat vegetable oil in a deep frying pan or kadhai over medium-low heat. Once the oil is hot, carefully add the dough balls to the oil, a few at a time. Fry them on low heat, stirring gently and continuously, until they turn golden brown and evenly

colored on all sides. Make sure the temperature of the oil is not too high, as it can brown the balls quickly without cooking them thoroughly.
6. Remove the fried balls from the oil using a slotted spoon and drain them on paper towels to remove excess oil.
7. In a separate saucepan, combine sugar, water, crushed cardamom pods, and saffron strands (if using). Bring the mixture to a boil, stirring occasionally to dissolve the sugar completely.
8. Once the sugar has dissolved and the syrup comes to a boil, reduce the heat to low and let it simmer for 5-7 minutes until it slightly thickens. Add rose water or kewra water (if using) and stir well.
9. Turn off the heat and gently drop the fried dough balls into the warm sugar syrup. Let them soak in the syrup for at least 1-2 hours, allowing them to absorb the sweetness and flavors of the syrup.
10. Serve Gulab Jamun warm or at room temperature. They can be enjoyed on their own or with a scoop of vanilla ice cream for a delicious dessert.

Enjoy the indulgent sweetness of homemade Gulab Jamun!

Prawn Curry

Ingredients:

- 500g prawns, cleaned and deveined
- 2 onions, finely chopped
- 2 tomatoes, finely chopped
- 3-4 garlic cloves, minced
- 1-inch piece of ginger, grated
- 2 green chilies, slit (adjust to taste)
- 1 teaspoon mustard seeds
- 1 teaspoon cumin seeds
- 1/2 teaspoon turmeric powder
- 1 teaspoon red chili powder (adjust to taste)
- 1 teaspoon ground coriander
- 1/2 teaspoon garam masala
- Salt to taste
- 2 tablespoons vegetable oil or ghee
- Handful of fresh cilantro leaves for garnish

Instructions:

1. Heat vegetable oil or ghee in a large skillet or pan over medium heat. Add mustard seeds and cumin seeds. Let them splutter.
2. Add finely chopped onions to the skillet and sauté until they turn golden brown.
3. Add minced garlic, grated ginger, and slit green chilies to the skillet. Sauté for another 2-3 minutes until fragrant.
4. Add chopped tomatoes to the skillet and cook until they become soft and mushy.
5. Stir in turmeric powder, red chili powder, ground coriander, garam masala, and salt. Mix well and cook for 2-3 minutes to let the spices toast and release their flavors.
6. Add the cleaned prawns to the skillet and mix well with the spice mixture. Cook for 5-7 minutes until the prawns turn pink and are cooked through.
7. Once the prawns are cooked, garnish with fresh cilantro leaves before serving.
8. Serve the Prawn Curry hot with rice, naan bread, or roti.

Enjoy your flavorful and aromatic Prawn Curry! Adjust the spiciness according to your taste preferences.

Chicken Vindaloo

Ingredients:

- 500g chicken, cut into pieces
- 2 onions, finely chopped
- 3 tomatoes, finely chopped
- 4-5 garlic cloves, minced
- 1-inch piece of ginger, grated
- 2 green chilies, slit (adjust to taste)
- 2 tablespoons vegetable oil
- 1 tablespoon mustard seeds
- 1 teaspoon cumin seeds
- 1 teaspoon turmeric powder
- 2 tablespoons red chili powder (adjust to taste)
- 1 tablespoon ground coriander
- 1 teaspoon ground cumin
- 1/2 teaspoon ground cinnamon
- 1/2 teaspoon ground cloves
- 1/2 teaspoon ground cardamom
- 1/4 cup vinegar
- Salt to taste
- Fresh cilantro leaves for garnish

Instructions:

1. Heat vegetable oil in a large skillet or pan over medium heat. Add mustard seeds and cumin seeds. Let them splutter.
2. Add finely chopped onions to the skillet and sauté until they turn golden brown.
3. Add minced garlic, grated ginger, and slit green chilies to the skillet. Sauté for another 2-3 minutes until fragrant.
4. Add chopped tomatoes to the skillet and cook until they become soft and mushy.
5. Stir in turmeric powder, red chili powder, ground coriander, ground cumin, ground cinnamon, ground cloves, and ground cardamom. Mix well and cook for 2-3 minutes to let the spices toast and release their flavors.
6. Add the chicken pieces to the skillet and mix well with the spice mixture. Cook for 5-7 minutes until the chicken is browned.

7. Pour in vinegar and mix well with the chicken and spices. Allow the vinegar to cook off for a couple of minutes.
8. Add salt to taste and adjust the consistency of the curry by adding water if needed.
9. Cover the skillet and let the chicken simmer over low heat for about 20-25 minutes, or until the chicken is cooked through and tender.
10. Once the chicken is cooked, garnish with fresh cilantro leaves before serving.
11. Serve the Chicken Vindaloo hot with rice, naan bread, or roti.

Enjoy the spicy and tangy flavors of Chicken Vindaloo! Adjust the spice level according to your preference.

Chicken 65

Ingredients:

For Marinating Chicken:

- 500g boneless chicken, cut into bite-sized pieces
- 2 tablespoons yogurt
- 1 tablespoon ginger-garlic paste
- 1 teaspoon red chili powder
- 1/2 teaspoon turmeric powder
- 1 teaspoon garam masala
- 1 tablespoon lemon juice
- Salt to taste

For Coating:

- 3 tablespoons cornstarch
- 3 tablespoons all-purpose flour (maida)
- 1 tablespoon rice flour (optional, for extra crispiness)
- 1/2 teaspoon red chili powder
- Salt to taste

For Frying:

- Vegetable oil for deep frying

For Tempering:

- 2-3 green chilies, slit lengthwise
- 10-12 curry leaves
- 3-4 garlic cloves, minced
- 1-inch piece of ginger, julienned
- 2 tablespoons chopped cilantro leaves

- 1 tablespoon lemon juice
- Salt to taste

Instructions:

1. In a mixing bowl, combine chicken pieces with yogurt, ginger-garlic paste, red chili powder, turmeric powder, garam masala, lemon juice, and salt. Mix well, ensuring all chicken pieces are coated evenly. Marinate for at least 1 hour, preferably longer for better flavor.
2. In another bowl, prepare the coating mixture by combining cornstarch, all-purpose flour, rice flour (if using), red chili powder, and salt. Mix well.
3. Heat vegetable oil in a deep frying pan or kadhai over medium heat.
4. Take each marinated chicken piece and coat it evenly with the flour mixture, shaking off any excess.
5. Carefully drop the coated chicken pieces into the hot oil and fry in batches until they turn golden brown and crispy. Remove them from the oil using a slotted spoon and drain on paper towels to remove excess oil. Set aside.
6. In a separate pan, heat a little oil over medium heat. Add slit green chilies, curry leaves, minced garlic, and julienned ginger. Sauté for a minute until fragrant.
7. Add the fried chicken pieces to the pan and toss well with the tempered spices.
8. Sprinkle chopped cilantro leaves and drizzle lemon juice over the chicken. Toss again to coat evenly.
9. Adjust salt to taste and mix well.
10. Serve Chicken 65 hot as an appetizer or snack, garnished with additional cilantro leaves and lemon wedges if desired.

Enjoy the spicy and flavorful Chicken 65! Adjust the level of spiciness according to your preference.

Tomato Rasam

Ingredients:

- 2 ripe tomatoes, chopped
- 1/2 cup cooked toor dal (split pigeon peas)
- 2 cups water
- 1 teaspoon tamarind paste
- 1 teaspoon rasam powder
- 1/2 teaspoon turmeric powder
- Salt to taste

For Tempering (Tadka):

- 1 tablespoon ghee or vegetable oil
- 1 teaspoon mustard seeds
- 1 teaspoon cumin seeds
- 2-3 dried red chilies
- A pinch of asafoetida (hing)
- 8-10 curry leaves
- 2 cloves garlic, minced (optional)
- 1-inch piece of ginger, grated (optional)
- 2-3 green chilies, slit lengthwise
- 2 tablespoons chopped cilantro leaves for garnish

Instructions:

1. In a pot, combine chopped tomatoes, cooked toor dal, water, tamarind paste, rasam powder, turmeric powder, and salt. Mix well and bring the mixture to a boil.
2. Reduce the heat to low and let the rasam simmer for about 10-15 minutes, allowing the flavors to meld together and the tomatoes to break down.
3. In a separate small pan, heat ghee or vegetable oil over medium heat for tempering.
4. Add mustard seeds to the hot oil. When they start to splutter, add cumin seeds, dried red chilies, and asafoetida. Stir for a few seconds.

5. Add curry leaves, minced garlic, grated ginger, and slit green chilies to the pan. Sauté for another minute until the garlic turns golden and the spices release their aroma.
6. Pour the tempered mixture into the simmering rasam and mix well. Let the rasam simmer for a couple more minutes.
7. Turn off the heat and garnish with chopped cilantro leaves.
8. Serve Tomato Rasam hot as a soup or with steamed rice and your favorite side dishes.

Enjoy the comforting and aromatic flavors of Tomato Rasam! Adjust the level of spiciness according to your preference.